UND]

Janet Ganguli (née Ait   ht
up in a Quaker family,   'ss
fortunate at an early a   .ty
she trained as a nurse   ..., ...u then, in 1975, set off for
India. She remained there for ten years, working to improve health
care in a part of Bihar (now Jharkhand), until family commitments
brought her back to England. Janet continues to retain her links
with the village where she worked. She currently works with refugees
and asylum seekers, and is active in the peace movement. Her
husband, a doctor from India, works for the International Federation
of the Red Cross. They have three children.

Under an Indian Sky

Ten Years in a Bihar Village

JANET GANGULI

PENGUIN BOOKS

PENGUIN BOOKS
Published by the Penguin Group
Penguin Books India Pvt Ltd, 11 Community Centre, Panchsheel Park, New
Delhi 110 017, India
Penguin Group (USA) Inc., 375 Hudson Street, New York, NewYork 10014,
USA
Penguin Group (Canada), 10 Alcorn Avenue, Toronto, Ontario, Canada
M4V 3B2 (a division of Pearson Penguin Canada Inc.)
Penguin Books Ltd, 80 Strand, London WC2R 0RL, England
Penguin Ireland, 25 St Stephen's Green, Dublin 2, Ireland (a division of
Penguin Books Ltd)
Penguin Group (Australia), 250 Camberwell Road, Camberwell, Victoria
3124, Australia (a division of Pearson Australia Group Pty Ltd)
Penguin Group (NZ), cnr Airborne and Rosedale Roads, Albany, Auckland
1310, New Zealand (a division of Pearson New Zealand Ltd)
Penguin Group (South Africa) (Pty) Ltd, 24 Sturdee Avenue, Rosebank,
Johannesburg 2196, South Africa

Penguin Books Ltd, Registered Offices: 80 Strand, London WC2R 0RL,
England

First published by Penguin Books India 2005

The views and opinions expressed in this book are the author's own and the
facts are as reported by her which have been verified to the extent possible,
and the publishers are not in any way liable for the same.

Typeset in Sabon by Mantra Virtual Services, New Delhi
Printed by Baba Barkhanath Printers, New Delhi

To my mother, who first introduced me to India,

To my late father, who always encouraged me and urged me to 'write it down!',

To my brother, with whom I shared my first experience of India,

To my husband and children, Sushila, Annie and Huboo, who would not be part of my life if I had not set forth, and

To Debimaya and all my village friends.

Contents

Prologue

From 1975 onwards, I spent ten years living and working as a volunteer in a little village in Santhal Parganas, Bihar, now part of Jharkhand. It is a different world from the one I, an English nurse, was born and brought up in and have now returned to. It is a different world too for most city-bred Indians. Indeed, when I first worked in the village with Service Civil International, India (SCI) and we received Indian visitors, they often found the change—the slow pace of life, the stillness and silence, the smokey fire, the stones in the rice and the domestic chores—just as hard to adapt to as our Western visitors.

The poor majority of villagers do not have many of the things we take for granted in our lives: no electric light, no tap water, no sanitation, no transport, no telephone, no books, no television, no radio. Their life consists of unremitting hard physical work, carrying heavy loads—be it water from the well or stream, paddy from the fields or wood from the forest—and walking long distances, all on a basic, unvarying and inadequate diet. And there is the ever-present threat that things will get worse because of illness or death in the family, or because of storm or drought or theft. On the other hand there are positive aspects to their lives—a more leisurely sense of time, more serenity, more freedom, a better appreciation of small things which comes with having so little and a greater sense of community.

The transition from a large London hospital to a remote village with absolutely no medical facilities was not easy. Often I felt that my training was more of a handicap than a help as I was constantly made aware of my inability to live up to the standards of care I had been taught to strive for. I was conscious above all that it was I who had a great deal of learning to do.

There were doctors and chemist shops and a government primary health-centre in the local town, some twelve miles across the fields, and the nearest hospital was several hours' journey away. The nearest government tuberculosis centre was even further away. It wasn't just the distance and the trouble in getting there that was an obstacle for the villagers, however, but the need to pay—even for supposedly free government services. This was also true of the services provided by the village quacks; the difference was that the quacks came to the villager's home and would accept payment in kind (in paddy, timber, animals or even land) and on credit and were therefore more commonly resorted to. Quacks were more familiar, a part of the villager's world. Traditional methods of healing were also practised but there was lesser reliance on herbal remedies than on superstitious rituals aimed at exorcizing the evil spirits that caused illnesses. Apart from the reduced influence of quacks, in the thirty years since I first went to the village, the picture has not changed very much.

From the outset I wanted to be involved in more than treating patients. I wanted to help tackle the causes which gave rise to most of the complaints and illnesses I encountered. It wasn't long before I realized that the main problem was not the lack of medical facilities but the lack of food. And the lack of food arose from many interrelated factors such as scarcity of resources for cultivation, no irrigation facilities, lack of employment opportunities and the constant drain on what meagre resources there were from moneylenders, quacks, traditional ceremonies and corrupt officials. A concern for people's health leads one quickly into the realm of human rights and politics. This is no doubt true in any society, however much we try to compartmentalize our lives. But here this truth was hard to escape.

Lack of adequate food led to many of the diseases that I encountered as poor nutrition lowers resistance to infection and reduces the chances of recovery. Large numbers of patients came to the clinic and it became difficult to find the time to engage in other activities besides providing this necessary but mainly palliative care. However, the need to visit patients in their homes took me to the villages nearby and sometimes far afield, giving me the opportunity to learn about village life and the problems villagers face. It was a long time before I was able to start the all-important task, as I saw it, of training village health workers. Training the villagers themselves in health work was the key as I saw it. Apart from their medical role, they could be agents for change, fostering awareness of the factors that affect health and helping villagers gain more control over their lives.

I was joined in later years by Manan, a doctor from Calcutta. The clinic and health care continued to be the focus of our work but over the years we responded to their needs in other ways too. We helped them with vegetable and wheat production, tree planting, organizing an annual mela, pressurizing the government for more support and encouraged them to try and increase their meagre earnings. Although we no longer work directly with the villagers, these tasks have been continued by the village health workers. Through our work together the feeling has grown amongst the villagers over a wide area that they now have an organization to help them carry forward their aspirations. It is not something that has been imported or imposed from outside. It has remained small scale and modest in keeping with the villagers' way of life. The centre that grew out of our work is still housed in a mud building, relying on the villagers' labour for its repair and renewal after each monsoon.

When approaching work amongst the very poor as an outsider, there is a careful path to be taken between the two extremes of idealizing their simplicity, self-sufficiency and resilience on the one hand and the all-too-common assumption of our superior knowledge and status on the other. It was only through long and close contact with the poor themselves and through our work with them that we were able to gain a deeper understanding and a more balanced view. In this way our experience was not that of a typical non-governmental organization (NGO) many of which work from within the confines of the project enclave or are based in urban centres from where excursions out into the villages are made by jeep. Such brief or sporadic encounters are unlikely to give any great insights into the lives of the poorest. Sadly, many NGOs are far removed from the realities of poverty and often fail to reach those most in need.

We should not forget that poor villagers are not just statistics but people like you and me, and apart from the poverty that they share in common, there is as much variety of humankind among them as anywhere else in the world: the hardworking, the lazy, the shy, the outspoken, the honest, the devious, the intelligent and the dull, the improvident and the enterprising. Amongst the people with whom we worked, whether Santhal, Muslim, Hindu or Dalit, were all of these, though, in my experience, the positive characteristics almost always stood out.

Living in the village was not a hardship to me and it was

not a sense of self-sacrifice that kept me there so long. The people, the countryside, the tranquillity, the simplicity of the way of life and the importance of our work made up for any lack of comfort or convenience. I felt privileged to have such an opportunity though on many occasions I felt inadequate in face of the challenges that presented themselves. If I honestly consider how much we achieved it is not a great deal and it is as much our failures that come to mind as our successes. We made many friends, saved lives and introduced new ideas; and the village health workers we trained continue to do so. But the villagers' world remains much the same.

I

TO THE VILLAGE

Continental Journey

For as long as I can remember I was drawn to the idea of going to India. My mother was born there but was shipped back to England and separated from her parents at the age of two, just after the First World War. It was not generally considered healthy for the children of the British Raj to be brought up in India. I'm sure it was not healthy to be separated from one's parents at such a tender age either. My grandparents were in India for twenty-five years until my grandfather was forced to retire early due to ill health. Frequent bouts of malaria and asthma had taken their toll. He died in England long before I was born. I grew up with stories of India told to me by my mother—of my grandfather rescuing a child ill with plague after a village had been evacuated; and of being vaccinated himself many times in order to persuade reluctant villagers to get vaccinated too. There were even some stories of his encounters with ghosts as he lay awake at night coughing. Later on, I came to know of his kindliness and idealism and strong principles so that I could never entirely agree with those detractors of the Raj who paint a completely black picture of that period of Indian history. No doubt a great deal occurred that was bad. Indeed, the very fact that a people should be ruled by strangers from thousands of miles away was wrong. But there were individuals like my grandfather who worked with a genuine sense of service. At any rate, it was not only the Indians who suffered but those children who were left behind in England, and no doubt their parents too.

For all my 'Indian connection', my ideas of the country were vague and the ties I felt were sentimental in nature rather than based on any real knowledge or understanding. I bought a map of India with my pocket money for 7s 6p when I was fourteen but it was to be another ten years before I set off with it, by which time some of the names on the map had changed: East Pakistan had become Bangladesh and Ceylon had become Sri Lanka. In the meantime I had completed a degree, a nursing and midwifery training, and had attended a course of lectures on tropical diseases at the Institute of Hygiene and Tropical Diseases in London.

In those days the overland route to India was a well-trodden one, 'the hippy trail' as it was popularly known. The Shah had not yet been overthrown in Iran and the Russians had not yet invaded Afghanistan rendering the route unsafe for carefree wanderers. There had even been a bus which took you straight to Delhi from Victoria coach station in London in eight days—real travelling, not hopping on and off planes and waiting in airport lounges!

The pace of my three-week journey was somewhat more leisurely. We used public transport, commencing and concluding the trip by train. Various types of vehicles of greater or lesser roadworthiness were used in between. I was one of a motley group led by the charismatic Ashley who had made the trip innumerable times before, and knew the route, some friendly characters along it, and various hidden corners of it, like the palm of his hand.

We left Victoria station in London one cold winter morning at the beginning of 1975. When preoccupation with preparations for my journey gave way to the realization of my imminent departure into the unknown, I was suddenly filled with misgiving. The first stage of the journey was familiar enough and brought back memories of many a previous trip to the continent—the train, the ferry, the train again through Paris and beyond. I lay on my couchette listening to the names of familiar places called out by the station announcer; some of them had been my destination in past travels but this time I was travelling on.

*

The memories of the journey have become blurred and faded with time. But some remain clear. Istanbul—the fabulous Blue Mosque, the fresh-juice shops, the enormous, noisy cars, a Turkish bath (what do you do with your money-belt you have been advised never to be parted from?), a cheap hot meal of stew in a tiny eating place little more than a hut, then being whisked off by Ashley to another for the second course because the puddings were better there. After three days we left behind the hubbub of the city and travelled on across the Bosphorus into Asia. After a night on the bus we arrived at Trabzon. Disappointment, as it didn't match up to my idea of a lovely Black Sea resort. Shauna and I nearly got left behind there—O horror!—as our expected morning call did not happen and we emerged with sinking hearts into an empty hotel foyer. Fortunately the bus had only rounded one corner before we were missed. Soon we were climbing up icy roads with chains on the bus tyres; around us were breathtaking views of seemingly deserted expanses of snow-covered mountains. A timely puncture allowed our eyes to linger on the scene while nearby two horses attached to a sleigh munched in nose bags.

In Erzerum the cold was memorable. There were sheets, indeed mounds, of solid ice on the streets. How the poor and the animals must have suffered from the cold! Further on, in

Agri, I remember tiny crystals of ice sparkling in the air.

We crossed the border into Iran and went on a 'mystery tour' in Tabriz, which turned out to be a trip to a magnificent railway station which was visited by one train a day. In Tehran some of Jim's luggage was stolen on arrival when he took his eyes off it for a moment as we disembarked in the darkness. I accompanied him to the police station to file a report so that he could make an insurance claim. There was a group of frightened, blood-stained young men tied up in the middle of the room. This was not Dixon of Dock Green. It was as if we had glimpsed some hidden horror beneath a veil of normality.

I was puzzled by my first sight of a large ceiling fan at our hotel and wondered what could be the purpose of fixing a propellor to the ceiling. In the freezing cold the idea of a cooling device did not occur to me. I filled my plastic drinking water bottle with hot water to make it into a hot-water bottle in an effort to keep warm. It went very soft but mercifully remained intact. Outside there were vendors with glowing braziers on the pavements and ovens which looked like holes in the wall where you could buy freshly baked hot bread.

We continued our journey to Mashad, with its wide streets and mosques, their walls covered with wonderful, elaborate mosaics and then on towards the Afghan border. While scrutinizing my Afghan visa in preparation for presenting it at the border, I realized to my alarm that it had been misdated and, according to the English version of the stamp on it, was out of date. Ashley suggested I return alone to Mashad to get another one which I was very loath to do. So we devised another plan. For the last part of the journey to the border, we squeezed into a taxi. I sat at the back. The border official looked at each passport in turn, given to him open at the visa page. When he had returned one to the girl in front she put it into a bag and passed it to me. When my turn came I took it out, opened it at the visa page and handed it to the official. I was terrified that he would turn to the photo page and see it was not me. But he was satisfied with a glance at the visa. Perhaps my relief added to my immediate liking of the place, with the gaily painted lorries and scruffy officials. Our cronky minibus surprisingly made the journey to Herat in two hours without mishap. The road had been built three years earlier. Up until then it had apparently taken up to eleven hours. We arrived just after dark and were greeted by the jingle of horses' bells in the dimly lit streets.

Herat was the highlight of the journey. The wide streets were easy to cross—how different from Tehran! Horses, decorated all over with red tassels, laden donkeys and camels passed down streets lined with quaint wooden buildings. Inside the dwellings were cosy and carpeted. Each room in our hotel had a stove for which we had to buy our own wood. But the poverty of the people was all too obvious. Many were pitifully dressed. Did I really see children barefoot on the frozen ground? I believe I did.

The bus ride to Kandahar took us through beautiful flat sandy plains with jagged mountains in the distance, looking almost as if they had been cut out of cardboard. We saw only a handful of vehicles on the road all day. Lines of camels, groups of rounded mud huts, and the occasional rather incongruous avenue of pine trees broke the monotony of the landscape.

Some elegant, balconied buildings in Kandahar were evidence of its colonial past. But my memory of Kandahar is mainly of falling into conversation with an educated local man in a restaurant and being encouraged to stay there to work as a much-needed nurse. I wonder what happened to him in the turbulent years that have followed in that tragic country.

One of my abiding memories of the journey is of the drive

from Kandahar to Kabul. I believe there had been a mix-up with the booking. At any rate, we made the eight-hour trip in a very old, rattling bus. There was no heating and the ill-fitting windows and doors let in icy draughts. The only way I could find to ease the pain in my cold feet in the sub-zero temperatures was to sit on the back of the seat—which meant keeping my head bowed—with someone sitting on them! We eventually arrived to be ushered into our hotel room and see panes of glass missing from the window. At this point the need to conserve funds quickly gave way to the more pressing need for some warmth and comfort. Jim, Shauna and I found another hotel nearby for not a great deal more with a fire and hot shower. Luxury!

While in Kabul, I looked up an acquaintance of my mother's who worked for the World Health Organization (WHO) there. This was to be my first experience of the comfortable lifestyle of those who worked for the UN and indeed of most expatriates. That is not to say that after all the rough travelling and the cold we didn't appreciate the Danish bacon, French cheeses and the cognac with which I and two of my co-travellers were generously entertained. It was fun too to travel in the chauffeur-driven WHO jeep. But at the same time it didn't feel quite right.

We travelled onward from Kabul to the pleasant and verdant town of Jalalabad and crossed the spectacular and forbidding Khyber Pass where, for a terrifying moment, the jeep we were travelling in started rolling backwards towards an abyss for some reason. The crowds and chaos of Peshawar were overwhelming. I saw my first leper and was shocked to see what I thought was a dead body lying on a wooden bed covered in a sheet from head to foot, until I realized it was just someone sleeping undisturbed by the flies! I quickly sought the refuge of my hotel room. By now I was travel-weary and impatient to reach our destination.

As we walked across the border into India the sun glinted through an avenue of tall trees and a man in a brightly coloured turban said, 'Welcome.'

*

Now that I have become so accustomed to life in India, it is not easy to recapture the reactions and emotions of my first days there. But I remember that in some ways things had an unexpected familiarity about them. Perhaps it was because the further I travelled, the stranger and more different I expected things to become. Perhaps it was the legacy of the country's colonial past, the English language or the Cadbury's chocolate bars. There was, of course, much that was completely new, evoking a myriad of emotions, some pleasant, others less so.

I met my brother in Delhi and we travelled around India together for two months. We mastered the art of making train reservations and jostled on station platforms to find our name on the list, marvelling at the cheapness of the fares (only five pounds from Calcutta to Madras, a journey of about thirty-three hours) and the multitude of passengers. We debated an appropriate response to the beggars, enjoyed the friendly curiosity of fellow passengers, survived the inevitable tummy upset and endured the crowds of onlookers who gathered round to watch as we deliberated our next move. Every day we woke up to 'another lovely day'.

We travelled to Calcutta where men pulled rickshaws and strained against carts piled high with heavy loads and where people washed in the gutter from overflowing broken hydrants. Stagecoaches, loaded with people and belongings, had wheels that looked as if they would collapse any minute. Cows with terrified calves, their umbilical cords still dangling, were driven chaotically through the traffic. Beggars displayed grotesque deformities while members of the Calcutta jockey club exercised their immaculate beasts in the dawn mist and rich ladies in sumptuous sarees stepped out from their chauffeur-driven cars to buy confectionery from Flurys in Park Street. We saw the domed edifice of the Victoria Memorial silhouetted dramatically against a blazing sunset.

In Puri I lost count of all the temples we were taken to see. In Cochin, where tall arched fishing nets stood out against the skyline, I thought I would imminently expire from the heat. In Goa we relaxed blissfully in the warm sea within sight of dolphins; and in the Nilgiris we travelled up from the sweltering plain into the cool of the mountains, with the scent of the eucalyptus trees amid slopes covered with tea plantations and attractive cosy-looking bungalows dotted here and there. In Kerala we accomplished part of our journey by boat through the tranquil waterways lined with coconut palms. Such vast distances and the varied climate, terrain and culture held together, it seemed, by the common use of English and the network of the railway.

Apart from absorbing all these new experiences, my purpose was to find a niche for myself to settle down in and start work. While in Delhi I had been in touch with the Indian branch of an international humanitarian organization that I had previously worked for in Europe called Service Civil International (SCI). In the course of our travels we visited several projects including one in a small village called Titmoh in Bihar that was run by this organization. It was to Titmoh that I decided to return.

2

Being 'Memsahib'

The SCI project had grown out of relief work undertaken at the time of the Bihar famine in the 1960s. It was an agricultural project though there was also an informal scheme to distribute medicines to the villagers. Two walled kitchen gardens had been established and divided between the villagers, each irrigated by means of a Persian wheel from an enormous well. A feeding programme took place every day. A large pan of khejuri was prepared on a wood fire beneath a mango tree by an elderly but very active village woman we called Mama, and a line of children, bowl in hand, queued up for their share at the appointed time. In the evenings a few children came to a night school and sat on the floor with their slates around a noisy pressure lamp to learn to read and write.

There were two other volunteers—Meindert, a Dutch agriculturalist, and Sreenivas from south India. Meindert was a tall, friendly young man with an analytical turn of mind. Sreenivas was neat and efficient with charming manners. The three of us lived simply in a mud house beside the mango tree, and drew our water from the well like the rest of the villagers. Unlike them, however, we had a simple, brick bathroom and toilet (not an example of superior hygiene until I prevailed upon my fellow volunteers to have a proper one built with a septic tank) and we had our firewood delivered by the cartload. We also had more food, better clothes and bedding, a plentiful supply of kerosene for our lamps (there was no electricity) and luxuries such as tea, sugar, soap and matches.

The nearest town of Madhupur was twelve miles away as the crow flies but the usual route was via the village of Jagdishpur. It was a five-mile walk across the fields to Jagdishpur and from there a train or bus ride to Madhupur. The town was on the main Calcutta–Delhi line, Calcutta being about six hours' journey to the east and Delhi twenty hours to the west. The prospect of living in a remote village was quite a daunting one, though the knowledge that European volunteers had lived there before me made it less so. I could not, of course, speak the local language. It took me a long time before I could speak it with any degree of fluency, hampered by the fact that the villagers spoke a dialect of Hindi called 'Khota' which was not in any books and had a good deal of Bengali mixed in as we were near the Bengal border. The tribal people spoke their own language, Santhali, which was completely different. Most Santhali men spoke Khota too but few of the women did.

The area had a mixed population comprising tribal people; Koles and Pujars (Dalits); Ghutvals (caste Hindus); and Muslims. Within Titmoh itself there were groups of Ghutvals, Koles, Pujars and Muslims, and the Santhal village of Jeromoh was just a short distance away. Only a few families were better off than the rest. The majority from all the groups were united in their poverty and each day was a struggle to survive.

Opposite us lived Dumnamaya, a Ghutval, in a little one-roomed hut with a leaky thatched roof. She had been married off before adolescence to a man a good deal older than herself. Her husband being so much older had saved her widowed mother from the necessity of providing an expensive dowry. Her dowry had consisted of a water pot and a plate.

Dumnamaya had found herself little more than a girl with a strange man many miles from her former home. By the time I arrived in the village she had a small son called Dumna. (Hence her name Dumnamaya or Dumna's mother.) When we first met she was very shy. Life was extremely hard for her—her husband either from ill health or inclination, or a combination of both, did not do much work. He was happy to sit around at home. The main burden of providing for her family and keeping them alive fell on her.

In the course of time I managed to get used to sitting on the hard floor and mastered the art of pulling water from the well without slopping half of it back inside. I learned how to wash my clothes by soaping them and banging them on the bathroom floor, how to clean lamp glass and trim wicks, how to eat rice with my fingers and how to wind a saree around me. It was a good deal harder though to get used to the lack of privacy and lack of any sense of timing on the part of the villagers. Patients would often assemble before I was up and sometimes come and sit in the yard outside my door in the early morning sunlight. I could hear them talking and see them through the cracks in the door. I would lament my inability to get up early and would have to brace myself to open the door and cross the yard to the bathroom with their eyes upon me.

The villagers called me 'memsahib'. Although I did not feel like a memsahib, I accepted what they wanted to call me. Later some called me 'ma' or 'Jan'.

Not very long after my arrival, I fell seriously ill, probably with dengue fever. My temperature soared and I lay on my plank bed racked with pain in my head and limbs, hardly able to move or eat for several days. It was embarrassing that patients should be sent away because 'memsahib', who was apparently here to help them be healthy, was ill herself. On the other hand it is good for a nurse to know what it feels like to be really ill. I slowly began to regain my strength and eventually re-emerged from my little room.

The villagers were already in the habit of coming to the centre for medicine and it was not long before I was busy with patients coming for treatment with complaints ranging from scabies and diarrhoea to TB and leprosy. Most of the examinations took place outside as it was too dark inside. The medicines were kept in a tin trunk. I soon had to get used to patients coming only when their complaint had reached a very advanced stage—their level of tolerance coupled with their lack of resources often meant they delayed seeking treatment till the last minute. Some didn't come at all. I would come across very sick people in the villages and wonder why they had never come for treatment. When I was unsure of the diagnosis I used to make arrangements to take the patients to a doctor in Madhupur but often they would not turn up. Sometimes, when I asked them to return for further treatment they didn't come back which was very frustrating, though I came to understand that this usually meant they were better. Seeing the patients recover was very satisfying but I sometimes had the feeling they might have recovered anyway!

I frequently felt a sense of inadequacy in treating the patients who came to me. In addition to this was the ever-present sense that what I was doing was palliative—I was not doing anything to change the conditions which were at the root of most of the diseases I was treating. But for the first two to three years it was hard for me to do anything other than spend most of my time treating or trying to treat the patients who came to me.

In doing so I made many friends, picked up a little of the local language and a good deal about the villagers' way of life and the meaning of poverty. I saw a child carefully and intently pick up a few grains of wheat that had spilled and shyly accept a plain biscuit with wondrous delight. I trailed through monsoon mud to a 'hospital' only to find that it was merely an empty shell of a building and I witnessed the activities of a 'doctor' whose real skill lay in prising money and possessions from his panic-stricken patients. I experienced the callous indifference and corruption of government officials. And I saw my bright, playful little neighbour Dumna die in front of my eyes.

It happened so quickly, in just a few hours. Dumnamaya was out collecting firewood and her husband, Jailal, came to tell me Dumna had a fever. I gave him some medicine and sat down to sponge and fan him. Meanwhile Dumnamaya came home exhausted and lay down on the floor of the hut and went to sleep. Little Debi (by now Dumna had a little sister) sat on the bed beside Dumna and helped me to fan him. Soon I realized to my horror he was not sleeping but unconscious. It was like a bad dream. Suddenly Dumnamaya was wide awake and there was a crowd of anxious villagers around the bed. I tried to resuscitate him but it was hopeless.

Dumnamaya was very brave. Her words reflected no bitterness but a profound weariness with the unending struggle to survive which only her children made worthwhile. During the days that followed, Debi would sometimes abruptly stop what she was doing and call 'Mana, Mana' (she couldn't say Dumna) and then wander unsteadily down the track past the well to look for him. Now Dumnamaya's name became 'Debimaya'.

In spite of the suffering, the poverty and frustrations, the place held a captivating charm for me. The sunshine and the tranquil beauty of the countryside restored my spirit. I felt a sense of determination to continue to try and establish something with the villagers which would be of lasting benefit to them. I took a break and went back to England for a few months. On arrival I experienced a culture shock much greater than when I had arrived in India. We lived near a big hospital and every time I heard the sound of an ambulance, I would stop what I was doing and my mind would go back to my village friends for whom there was no ambulance and no hospital. I returned to Titmoh in the spring of 1978. I started working independently now and lived alone, renting a little room in a widow's house which served as bedroom, kitchen, clinic and classroom!

I held meetings in other nearby villages and asked the villagers to select one of their number to train as a village health worker. I started training five of them, four men and one woman. They had a small monthly allowance and a box to keep their medicines in. Each had a number of villages under his or her care. I gradually introduced them to the basics of health care and trained them to diagnose and treat common complaints, while slowly building up their proficiency in administering medicine and advising on health care. At the same time, having prepared a series of lessons for children, I visited village schools in the area to talk to them about matters relating to health.

Early in 1980 I attended a gathering of medical professionals which took place at a big health project in Maharashtra. There I met Manan, a young Bengali doctor from Calcutta. He was selling a radical magazine called *Health and Society*, which he edited himself. I bought a copy and we talked about my village work. He said he would visit me.

One evening, a few weeks later, when everyone including myself had gone to bed, there was a sound of voices in the darkness and a knock at the door. It was Manan. The Calcutta train had been late again. After waiting some hours in Madhupur and not realizing I lived in such a remote place, he had continued his journey to Jagdishpur only to find, to his surprise, the place shut up and deserted. He was advised to return to Madhupur for the night. However, undeterred, he had eventually contrived to persuade someone to bring him to Titmoh in the dark.

He stayed for a few days in the village and found it a strange contrast to Calcutta. He said he felt as if life here was lived in slow motion. When patients came, it was heartening to see the care and friendliness with which he examined and treated them. He went back to Calcutta to finish his hospital duties and decided to return to Titmoh.

It was like a dream come true to have support and companionship, and a competent and caring doctor. The work now had a much stronger basis on which to build upon. In deciding to come and work in the villages, Manan was giving up the chance of furthering his medical career. One of his friends said to me, 'Here's an idealistic doctor, one in a thousand, and you want to take him off to a village where he won't be able to change anything!' I also was not without misgivings on his account but Manan did not appear to have any such doubts. By now the SCI project had closed down and we were able to move back to the house beside the mango tree.

At the beginning of the 1980s there was a series of disastrous harvests and the villagers' already precarious food supplies dwindled further, plunging them into a crisis. One evening I found Debimaya and her family eating unripe custard apples. That was all they had. Manan and I felt it was the government's duty to take action. When, after several attempts and applications, nothing happened, we saw this as an opportunity to raise the villagers' awareness and prompt them to act together in pursuit of their rights. In this we were very successful. Hundreds of villagers marched on the government offices. A new spirit had grown amongst them. Debimaya became very active and militant, a far cry from the shy, timid girl I had first met. We found it moving and inspiring. The authorities reacted by making allegations and threats against us. The threats were particularly directed against me as a foreigner. An article appeared in the local press entitled, 'Foreign girl misguiding labour force'. As my position was becoming more vulnerable, it seemed an appropriate time to get married. By now Manan's parents, who had been surprisingly tolerant of his move to the villages, had become used to the idea of having an English daughter-in-law. Our Bengali wedding in Calcutta was followed by one in Titmoh where my village friends, Hindu, Dalit, Muslim and Santhali all joined hands to dance together.

The villagers' demonstration was a watershed in other ways. It showed us the potential for collective action that lay beneath the villagers' apparently passive exterior and it helped pave the way for the building of the villagers' centre. The centre was built in the Santhal village of Fatepur, about a mile from Titmoh. We called it 'Ekta Niketan', home of unity. We moved to Fatepur and by then we had a little daughter, Sushila. She was much admired and thrived in the outdoors. As she grew older she effortlessly absorbed four languages which she mixed together. She enjoyed excursions on the back of my bicycle, chasing hens, chewing on tamarind from the tree beside our house, and enthusiastically helped in spreading the mud to renew the floors and walls.

We left the village in 1986 when Sushila was three years old. Since then the villagers have continued the work. It never was and never will be a large project, let alone an institution. Rather, it is an experiment which aims at fostering confidence among the villagers to work together for a better life.

*

When we who are lucky to have a reasonably comfortable life and more than sufficient to eat realize that a huge number of people in the world are poor and lack the basic prerequisites of a healthy life, the solution at first might appear to be to get there and set up feeding programmes, hospitals, clinics,

irrigation facilities and seed banks. As if poverty is a hole
you have to fill. I remember seeing films when I was young
which reinforced this idea. One particularly impressed me—
it showed how a test had identified the lack of a particular
substance in the soil and once the missing element was added,
the crops grew miraculously strong and plentiful. To the
sound of triumphant music, we saw barren land transformed
into fields of healthy wheat extending into the distance. By
the time I reached Titmoh I had already realized that improving
the lives of the poor was not so simple.

I believed the way was through education and the
imparting of appropriate knowledge and skills. 'Give a man
a fish and you feed him for a day. Teach a man to fish and
you feed him for life.' So, for example, I saw no long-term
benefit in the feeding programme but, since it was happening,
sought to use it as an opportunity to encourage in the children
the habit of washing their hands before they ate. I composed
a series of 'health messages' which if followed, I believed,
would improve the people's health. I had yet to understand
that they were the experts in living and surviving in poverty
not me; that if there were any fish around, you could be
pretty sure the locals would know how to catch them and
wouldn't need to be taught.

Over the course of time I came to understand that just as
poverty did not simply signify the lack of material things,
nor could its cause be found in the people's ignorance. What
the poor lacked was justice and the power to control their
own lives.

3

Madhupur: Gateway to Another World

As the train left behind the coconut palms and banana trees surrounding dark ponds, rice fields and lush greenery of West Bengal, the land slowly rose. The steam engines were changed at Asansol near the Bengal–Bihar border and strained as the gradient gradually increased. The land became drier and sandier, the vegetation more sparse. About two hundred miles west of Calcutta, the train rattled across a bridge spanning a wide sandy river bed and soon after this drew into the small market town of Madhupur.

Madhupur was like the crossover point between our world and the world of the village folk. The villagers occasionally came to Madhupur on market days to sell their leaf plates and other produce, and to make small purchases. The inhabitants of Madhupur however seldom ventured into the villages.

Madhupur was a pleasant, quiet town, if a little shabby. Due to its proximity to Calcutta and its more favourable climate, it had long been a holiday resort for middle-class Bengalis during the pujas and the winter months. They were called 'changers' and arrived with their bedrolls, trunks, tiffin cans, colourful woollies and Kashmiri shawls. The ill-clad villagers looked on with curiosity. Many of the large, ornate houses in spacious grounds on the outskirts of the town were owned by Bengalis who lived in Calcutta. They remained empty for most of the year, some in an advanced state of decay. Like remnants of a past age, they evoked a strange and nostalgic sense of lost grandeur. The shutters would be down, trees growing out of the brickwork, a lone figure—maybe the caretaker—crouched on the steps, and a few goats would be browsing in the overgrown garden, having entered from the gap where a part of the garden wall had fallen down. A picture of abandonment and quiet desolation so different from the vibrancy and activity in the town just a little distance away.

There was not a great deal of note in the town—a few cottage industries making candles, soap, bidis and tin trunks, a glass factory, a catholic mission school, a leprosy hospital and a rundown hotel called The Raj. The grocery, hardware, cloth and chemist shops drew their custom from the many villages around and the town was packed on Mondays and Fridays, the market days. The fruit and vegetable sellers set up their colourful stalls on the market-place grounds under a big banyan tree.

Till just a few years ago a jeep or car was an uncommon sight amongst the cycle rickshaws, bicycles and tongas pulled by small, thin, sad-eyed ponies. They drove at walking pace, honking their way through the narrow, crowded streets in the centre of the town past vendors squatting by the roadside in front of the open drain selling rope, bamboo baskets, chillies, colourful glass and plastic bangles, toys, trinkets and hair braids, and earthen water pots of different shapes and sizes. There were tailor shops where the workers bent industriously over their sewing machines, and bright saree shops where the customers sat on the floor to examine and select their purchase. And often blaring over everything from a loudspeaker was the all-pervasive sound of Hindi film music. Each week a man on a tonga would go around town, loudly announcing the current film showing at the cinema to the accompaniment of shrill dialogues of the hero and heroine. The songs from Hindi films are far more evocative of India to me than the sound of tabla and sitar.

A trip to Madhupur would often include a visit to the bank. It was not a good idea to go to the bank unless you had a great deal of time on your hands. Unfortunately this was usually not the case. Even a fairly simple transaction would involve waiting in several different queues one after the other as your passbook made painfully slow progress from a pile on one desk to the next and the clerks leisurely made their entries into various ledgers. At some point during the proceedings one was handed a token and when, at long last, you exchanged the token for the return of your passbook you couldn't help feeling a sense of achievement. I used to find it hard to maintain my patience as the hours ticked by and tried various ways of dealing with it without much success. One was to get friendly with the bank manager. This resulted in a chair being offered and perhaps a cup of tea and a chat but didn't necessarily expedite matters. Another was to go off and do some shopping once I had accomplished the token stage. On bad days I just lost my temper. Unfortunately that seemed to work best.

Another port of call was the chemist. Although we bought most of our drugs in bulk, we sometimes needed more supplies. It was a sobering lesson in the state of health care to observe and to listen to what went on in the chemist shops. Many patients—or, more often, the patient's relatives—came straight to the chemist, described the symptoms and bought medicines without the patient ever being examined. When patients did come with a prescription they often wouldn't be able to afford all the medicines on it and so would leave some out—maybe the most important one—or not buy the full quantity, even of antibiotics.

When I first came to Madhupur there were three doctors there that I knew of including a government doctor. This number increased substantially over the years. In theory government doctors were not supposed to charge for consultation, but in practice they did. Their income was further enhanced by the sale of government medicines meant for free distribution. At various times in the years before Manan came to work in the village, I would, on occasion, try and enlist their help in the diagnosis of patients' ailments and the supply of drugs (in particular chloroquine against malaria, iron tablets for pregnant women and contraceptive pills). There was never any shortage of condoms; they were obviously not a saleable item.

Off a wide road, leading eastwards out of town, there was a hospital with the rather unappealing name 'Reconstructive Surgery Leprosy Hospital'. The locals called it 'Kodai Hospital' or leprosy hospital. I usually took a cycle rickshaw to go there. I never got used to the idea of someone expending their physical energy and sweat to convey me along and it made me feel odd and self-conscious, but the rickshaw drivers' obvious enthusiasm to earn some money in this way helped to relieve my qualms. On the way there, we would pass a large well where men would be busy drawing water and carrying it to nearby shops and houses in buckets and large tin cans hanging from a bamboo pole resting on their shoulder. There was no mains water supply in Madhupur—this was so even years later, after the construction of an impressive water tower. The road was wide but only the middle bit was metalled. Drivers of the dilapidated, overcrowded buses would honk frantically to make the rickshaw move out of their way and would screech past, raising clouds of dust in the summer and muddy splashes in the rainy season.

The hospital stood in the centre of a large, pleasant, well-tended garden surrounded by a high wall and, with broad steps leading up to the entrance, it had more the air of a grand country residence (which it probably used to be) than a hospital. The hospital had an X-ray machine, the only one in Madhupur, and so it was here, at the beginning, that we brought the patients we suspected of having TB for a chest X-ray. It was run by a voluntary organization. Rumour had it that it was really a front for the local businessmen involved in it to avoid taxation.

My friend Choudhary ran a grocery shop. It had an open frontage—as many shops did—and was raised above the level of the road with steps leading up to it. Inside, there was a seat to one side, where one could sit in the comfort of the ceiling fan (when there was not a power cut, as there frequently was) and watch the world go by. On the road below, labourers would strain up the hill like beasts of burden, pulling a slatted wooden cart full of sacks, which they would then, bent double, unload on to their backs to deliver to the mill opposite. In front of the mill, women squatted selling *sattu* (ground, roasted gram) and *datwan* (twigs used for cleaning teeth).The labourers and others would buy sattu, mix it with water in a leaf plate and eat it with some salt and a chilli as a nutritious and satisfying instant meal. The women weighed it out with hand-held scales using stones as weights. One old woman sat there so long day after day, I used to wonder if it was possible for her to stand up straight. Occasionally they had to shoo away the cows and goats that roamed freely on the streets.

Inside Choudhary's shop, at the centre were sacks filled with various types of rice and lentils, and also white sugar, jaggery, wheat flour and salt. Most things were sold loose and had to be weighed and packed into bags that Choudhary had carefully made himself out of newspaper or old exercise-book pages sealed with homemade flour-and-water paste. Customers would take a sample of rice in the palm of their hand to examine it. Even biscuits could be bought loose. Mustard oil and peanut oil for cooking, and kerosene oil for lamps and stoves, were measured out and poured into customers' bottles using a funnel. The villagers' little glass bottles often had a stopper fashioned out of a leaf and a piece of string around their neck to hold them by. Women kept their few coins and rolled-up notes tied in a knot in the corner-edge of their sarees. Many people could only afford small quantities of the wares. The village women would come in the morning after selling their leaf plates and Choudhary would quickly measure out their small amounts of kerosene, cooking oil and salt before they set off hurriedly to catch the train home.

On the shelves and in the glass-fronted cupboards along the walls of the shop were jars of spices, various brands of soap, detergent, matches, candles, lamp wicks, batteries, tins of hair oil, milk powder, jars of instant coffee and packets of tea. Choudhary didn't have a fridge so if there was any butter it was kept at his brother's chemist shop. Goddess Lakshmi looked down on the scene from her frame on the wall. Every morning a priest came, for a small monthly fee, to deck the goddess with fresh flowers.

Choudhary was a great support and, in times of need, would put himself out to be helpful in spite of his busy day. His shop was a retreat, as much from the difficulties and frustrations I inevitably experienced in the course of my various activities, especially my encounters with officialdom and the 'kal aiye' (come tomorrow) syndrome, as from the heat of the street. I used to go there to let off steam; Choudhary used to say, in not a very complimentary way I thought, that I was like tin that heated up quickly only to cool down again quickly.

Another place of retreat was the station canteen which offered a variety of dishes. A long list displayed the menu in

Hindi and English (with some amusing spelling) in neat writing high on the wall. One could sit in comfort, writing letters and observing the comings and goings, and the eating habits and interactions of the various characters who passed through. Activity in the kitchen would reach a noisy crescendo when a train was due to arrive, and meals on trays were piled high and hurried out to the platform. The station also afforded the luxury of a basin with running water for washing sweaty hands and face and—if you could find the man with the key—a toilet in the first class ladies' retiring room. (I used to wonder how my village friends managed in this regard when in town until I realized the advantage of wearing long sarees without underwear.)

The railway station was indeed the hub of the town. Across the street were the two-storey yellow-coloured railway quarters and beside them the railway hospital. Further up the road, parallel to the railway line, were the large ponds from which the steam trains used to draw their water. The various sounds of the railway station—the whistling, the rattling, the shunting, the chuffing and the clanging—became very familiar to me when I rented a little house nearby.

After a particularly hectic spell in the village I decided I needed to remove myself for a time in order to take stock and plan the future of my work there. Although the demands made on me and the possibilities appeared limitless, my energy and abilities, naturally, were not. The little house I eventually rented for the remarkable sum of fifty rupees a month including electricity, was in the compound of a house owned by a very kindly retired Anglo-Indian gentleman, Mr O'Rourke. Like many Anglo-Indians he had worked with the railways. He had been the driver of a mail train on the Delhi–Howrah line, having worked his way up from cleaning wheels. He lived alone most of the time as his wife preferred to stay with their daughter in Calcutta and so he was glad for some company.

The house, which came to be known as the Mad Pad, consisted of two small rooms, a kitchen (with a table!) and a bathroom. It backed on to open fields and had a veranda overlooking the garden at the front. To the side was the two-storey Carmel Mission school, so the sounds from the station mingled with the sound of chanting children heard through the open classroom windows.

Saleem, the cheerful, enthusiastic young boy who fetched water for us, was from the Muslim quarter of the town nearby, Kalasi Mahalla. He would willingly fill up every receptacle in sight, full to the brim. He collected used batteries which he claimed he was able to breathe new life into though I'm not sure how. Once when he asked me what the time was and I said 4 o'clock, he replied: '*Aaj bahoot jaldi char baj gara, memsahib*! (How come it's four so early today!)' My landlord had an elderly Hindu cook, Bochi, who walked four and a half miles from his village and back each day. He was a quiet, gentle man. The grubbiness of his jacket did not diminish the sweetness of his smile or the excellence of his preparations. The friendship between the young Muslim boy and the elderly cook was one of many examples that demonstrated to me the lack of any inherent hostility between Hindu and Muslim.

Mr O'Rourke would spend most of the day sitting on his veranda listening to the radio and enjoying a grandstand view of the procession of vehicles (mainly bullock carts, bicycles and rickshaws), livestock and humanity that passed by on the road. From time to time he would exchange a cheery greeting as a friend came into view. Occasionally, he would take out his bicycle and ride into town to do some shopping or shut up house and go off to Calcutta to visit his wife and daughter. In the evenings he would be joined by fellow Anglo-

Indians and, from time to time, the Roman Catholic priest to gossip and play cards. Sometimes, when he had no visitors, I would join him. Sitting under the stars in the cool of the evening, partaking of something Bochi had prepared, chatting in English and listening to the BBC World Service, I felt a strange sense of detachment from the world around me and a confirmation of the never-ending variety of life in this land of contrasts.

4

Village Rhythms

As you walk up the slope northwards, away from Jagdishpur station, crunching discarded earthenware tea cups underfoot, you arrive at a row of higgledy-piggledy open-air tea stalls and small shops. Behind them are some dilapidated brick houses with a path alongside that leads to the road and the open countryside beyond. The road is not busy—only an occasional gaily painted lorry, a crowded bus, a private car, a jeep, a few bicycles and sometimes a bullock cart pass along it each day. In just a few moments one leaves behind the bustle and crowds of the station, the tea stalls and the shops and finds oneself looking out towards a different world.

Once you leave the made-up road, sandy paths lead off into the distance. The eye reaches across the gently undulating landscape to the horizon. Clusters of orange-coloured mud houses dot the countryside so it is often hard to say where one village ends and the next one begins. Here and there the dark leaves of the mahua, jackfruit and mango trees provide welcome shade while clumps of light-green, swaying bamboos provide homes to egrets, mynas, sparrows and snakes. Small children tend to the animals—cattle, goats and a few sheep. There are no fences so they have to take care that the animals do not stray. The villagers walk for miles and miles, mostly barefoot, and often carrying heavy loads on their head or shoulders. Here, a jeep or a motorbike or even a bicycle is a rare sight. Occasionally a bullock cart belonging to a better-off villager plods by, carrying a load of wood or manure or tiles, or paddy for milling.

Each stretch and each landmark on the walk between Jagdishpur and Titmoh became familiar to me. The path took one across flat, barren land with wide views, through areas covered by bushes and trees, over the raised bandhs between the paddy fields, down to the stream, through small hamlets and past a village pond with a line of tall palm trees standing like sentries until, beyond another belt of paddy fields, you could just see the clumps of bamboo and the mango tree beside which we lived.

Usually we would arrive back in the village in the evening, having come by the four o'clock train from Madhupur. Sometimes it was late and there would be concern about reaching home before dark. I would watch the red sun sinking into the horizon knowing that when it finally disappeared I had half an hour of daylight left, half an hour to get home before nightfall.

At this time the villagers and their herds attended by little boys are making their way homewards too. A few villagers stop by at the little village shop to buy some scoops of mustard oil in an old medicine bottle or a little salt wrapped in a leaf. There are gatherings beside the wells and streams as women fetch water for the evening meal. Fires are being lit. If the embers have gone out, more live embers from another house are fetched on a ladle and coaxed into flame. A layer of smoke hangs over the houses. The chattering egrets come back to roost in the bamboo tree. It is time to light the kerosene lamps. By the time the meal is over, it is nightfall and the small children fall asleep in a corner of a rope bed or on a bed of straw. Some murmuring of voices may be heard for a while as the men sit chatting, the end of their bidis glowing in the darkness. Then, having cleared up after dinner and made sure the sturdy wooden door is securely fastened, the adults join their sleeping children.

On those nights of the month when the moon is out, there is a welcome white light over the quiet countryside. It is then possible to move around freely. A moonless night is so dark that keeping your eyes open or closed is the same! Even the villagers, used to the darkness and familiar with the surroundings, get disoriented and lost when venturing further afield. In the darkness the star-studded sky is truly magnificent. In our world of electricity and ample lighting, we have diminished our ability to appreciate the splendour of the night sky.

Built from sun-baked earth, the little village dwellings blend with the countryside, their roofs either thatched with paddy straw or made from earthen tiles. The Santhali houses are more distinctive, with a wide seat around the base which is blackened with burnt straw and contrasts with the walls coated with pale mud. The Santhals take much pride in skilfully smoothing, levelling and angling the surfaces of the walls and the seat. Sometimes doorways are decorated with carved animals' heads, and floral and bird designs adorn the walls. On occasion a mirror is embedded in the wall. The doorway is low and there are no windows. During the day the doors remain open to let light into the dark interior which accommodates the family's few possessions—a rope bed or two, a small stool, some plates and cooking pots, a stone pestle and mortar, a bamboo winnower beside the stove, and an axe and a brush against the wall. In the dark recesses of the house are the barrels made of twisted paddy straw containing the family's paddy store. A tin trunk keeps a few garments safe from rats. In a corner inside or in the courtyard under an overhanging roof is the *denki*. This is a long, heavy beam one end of which is worked up and down by the foot while the hammer attached to the other end pounds the paddy in a hollow in the ground. This action separates the rice from the husk. The *thud thud* of the denki can often be heard during the winter months early in the morning, even before daybreak has wakened the cockerels.

The villagers' day begins early. At sunrise, as the cocks crow, the chickens and the pigs are let out and villagers disappear into the fields to answer the call of nature. The dishes from the previous night's supper are piled up and taken with a bucket to the well or the stream to be washed up. The water pots are filled and ablutions performed. (Teeth are cleaned with twigs one end of which is chewed to make a brush.) Courtyards are swept clean. Breakfast usually consists of some rice leftover from the day before which has been kept in water overnight. But in winter, when the mornings are cold and rice more plentiful, a hot meal is prepared.

The wells and streams are gathering places where the women wash their aluminium and brass pots and dishes, scouring them one by one with mud or ash and then dexterously pouring water over them to rinse them thoroughly, all to the accompaniment of their tinkling bangles. Some squat while others, particularly the Santhal women, bend down with straight legs and back, bottom in the air.

Some women and girls leave to go to the jungle to cut firewood or to gather leaves to make into leaf plates and grass to make brushes which they sell. Depending on the time of the year, the men leave for work if they have any. They set off to prepare land for cultivation, guiding the little wooden plough behind the bullocks and emitting strange grunts and exclamations as they do so. They level land to make paddy fields for better-off villagers; they dig the earth and knead it with their feet to mix it with water and turn it into mud to repair a house or build a new one; they tend vegetables or thresh paddy. The boys take the cattle and goats out to graze. At a young age they are in charge of the family's most valuable asset. Their task is particularly important at the time of year when there are crops growing in the fields. Sometimes they are not vigilant, and crops and vegetables are spoilt. Other children look after their younger brothers and sisters in their parents' absence. They play with sticks and stones on the sandy ground, climb trees and go off in search of wild fruit. The young and elderly remain at home. Some will work the denki, dehusking the paddy in preparation for the day's meal. They may give the floor a new coating of cow dung, spreading it methodically with a wide arc-like movement. Now and again the hens have to be shooed off the vegetable patch.

Some villagers belong to groups involved in a particular occupation. The Mahtoos keep cows and sell dahi and milk. The Pujars are potters, skilled in making earthenware water pots and tiles using a simple hand-operated wheel. The Mohlis are basket makers making winnowers and beautiful baskets of various types for storage and carrying. There are a few carpenters and blacksmiths. The occupation of the village midwife and 'jungli doctor' also passes from parent to offspring. In spite of providing a vital service these people remain, for the most part, very poor.

By midday the animals are brought home to drink and the women return with their heavy loads. It is time to rest a little and eat, usually a portion of rice with a little vegetable or lentils. Sometimes the villagers go down to the stream or to a pond to have a bath and to wash their clothes which are then spread out on the ground and rocks to dry. Often they have no change of clothing. When their clothes are dry they put them on again. In the afternoon the animals are taken out to graze once more and the women and children stay back and sit together outside making leaf plates. The leaves are skilfully pinned together with slithers of bamboo or neem twigs and put in the sun to dry. Later, in the evening, they are gathered up and put under a heavy stone to press them flat after which they are ready to be bundled up and taken to market.

Occasionally there are visitors—a bread seller on a bicycle ringing his bell, a pot seller with a huge basket of pots and pans balanced on his head, an itinerant barber, a holy man collecting donations of rice, a buyer of chickens or bamboo, a contractor looking for willing labourers. But many days can go by with little contact with the outside world.

5

Rail Links

For the most part the train was our link with the world
beyond the villages. It took us to Madhupur and further
afield and, occasionally, in the other direction to Giridih. A
train plied to and fro between Madhupur and Giridih, a
distance of some forty miles, four times a day on a single-
track branch line. It would leave on its first journey very
early in the morning and return on its last journey of the day
late in the evening. Jagdishpur was the last stop before
Madhupur.

Although the villagers themselves would think nothing
of walking the twelve or so miles to Madhupur and back
again, they also used the train. On market days, the women
with their long bundles of leaf plates would throng the
platform at Jagdishpur jostling to get on board as the train
drew into the platform. It was a steam train, a great and
powerful beast with so much more character and emotion
than the diesel that has now, sadly, replaced it. It reminded
me of the Thomas the tank engine stories by Reverend Awdry
of my childhood. There was a 'fat controller' in those stories.
The 'fat controller' in Madhupur was indeed a portly
gentleman. He was a kindly Bengali with a round face. One
day the driver of the Giridih train lost control and it crashed
into the station, killing him.

Sometimes I would take the train to Calcutta. It was

always a mind-blowing experience to be suddenly transported from the peace and tranquillity of the villages to the hubbub of the city. This was especially so when I caught the night train, leaving the quietness of the village as the sun dipped below the horizon and the colours faded, and arrived in Calcutta amid the morning rush. Suddenly one's senses and emotions were assailed from all sides.

The trains were often crowded. However, any discomfort at not finding a seat on the Madhupur train was offset for me by my apprehensions about the bedbugs of which I had discovered there were a considerable number within the slatted wooden seats. The crowds often made both getting on and off difficult and hazardous. In desperation I have sometimes been obliged to climb out of the window—on the wrong side of the track. Once an old man was brought to us, having fallen off a train. It was during the wedding season when the trains are particularly full. He had tried to get off the train before it had stopped so that he could help his family from whom he had become separated. He slipped on to the track. They arrived at nightfall, having carried him to us over the fields leaving a trail of blood. His leg had been cut through to the bone. Manan spent most of the night repairing the terrible wound by the light of a torch. Unfortunately, when it was time to stitch up the skin, he discovered that some was missing. The old man was amazingly stoical and uncomplaining. We decided to take him to a hospital which meant carrying him back across the fields to Jagdishpur. It was difficult to find any help—his relatives were preoccupied with the wedding. Eventually Manan himself helped carry him and we succeeded in admitting him to a mission hospital with the help of some missionary acquaintances of ours. He was given a skin graft and surprisingly, after several weeks of treatment, his leg was saved.

Another patient, Sudani, lost three fingers while retrieving a bundle of leaf plates which had fallen on to the line as she tried to escape a ticket collector. She came to me after four months, after having had some treatment, since the wound had not healed. A doctor in Madhupur told me the bone was probably infected and I took her for an X-ray to Deoghar. (The machine in Madhupur was broken at the time.) The X-ray technician, unaware of the real reason behind the absence of the fingers, informed me that she had leprosy. He asked if she was my servant and I answered no, I was her servant! She was a great character and very lively and talkative, so it was a great pleasure trying to help her. We went for a meal afterwards for which she was touchingly appreciative, saying in her strong dialect, 'One feels so much better after a good meal, doesn't one.'

An altercation between a ticketless student and a railway official at Madhupur station got seriously out of hand one day. The student was apparently beaten up. When his fellow students heard of this they came to the station and demanded to see their friend. This request was refused and, in response, they set about uncoupling the railway carriages and stopped the trains in both directions. In the meantime, unknown to the students, the railway police had called in reinforcements from the Bihar Reserve Police which arrived in the afternoon. True to form they opened fire into the crowd that had gathered in front of the station. In the atmosphere of panic and terror that followed it was difficult to gain an accurate picture of the number of casualties, but at least one innocent bystander, a milk boy, was killed. The town was put under curfew.

The crowded trains were, naturally, a magnet for all sorts of vendors, beggars, those trying to earn an honest living, and those making a dishonest one. The succession of visitors passing through the railway compartment helped break the tedium of a long journey—the blind singer, the sellers of peanuts, sweets, toys, boiled eggs and cold drinks, the shoeshine boy capable of making the most worn-out shoe look as good as new, the little sweeper boy, the young man selling *shonpopri* (a type of sweet) and the sellers of *littipani*— small thick nan bread stuffed with a tasty sauce which was washed down with large amounts of water kept in containers hung outside the carriage. One of my favourites though, was an old man who sold 'Tiger Balm', a sort of ointment containing menthol. He had a wonderful speech extolling the many curative properties of this preparation and it was funny to watch the reactions of the passengers as he solemnly applied a sample to their foreheads.

Whenever the train pulled into a station, the air would become alive with the vendors' cries. The most evocative was the ubiquitous cry of 'chai, chai'. Tea would be poured into a little earthen cup. At first I found it difficult to throw away these little cups and collected them under my seat to the amusement of fellow passengers, but in time I learnt to throw them away as nonchalantly as the next person. Later I was happy to find that some of these originated in a local village.

Beggars could be a problem. Actually it was not the beggars that were the problem, the problem was how you confronted your own feelings and reacted to them. Society seemed to be divided between those who gave to the beggars and those who did not. Accepted wisdom amongst tourists seemed to be not to give—no doubt to avoid the embarrassing and uncomfortable situation of giving some money to one beggar and promptly being surrounded by many more. The cynical, to add weight to their desire to shut out the problem, would argue that giving to beggars encouraged and condoned begging. While travelling around India my brother and I tried to solve the problem by dividing them into categories— children and able-bodied in the category for not giving and the old, the blind and the handicapped in another that one gave to. Sometimes, though, we would compromise and share our food with the children.

Apart from the vendors and the beggars there were, inevitably, those who would divest you of your money or possessions in a more devious fashion. At Jamtara station, not far from Madhupur, the watch snatchers had developed their act to a fine art. Just as the train was pulling out of the station, they would skilfully rip the watch from the wrist of the unsuspecting passenger who had unwisely rested his or her arm on the frame of the open window. On several occasions I have heard the shouts of dismay and commotion that followed but all to no avail, for the train was now picking up speed and the distance between the watch and owner was rapidly increasing. Another type of illicit activity that took place regularly on the Madhupur–Giridih line was the distribution of coal. A villager would hold up a stick with some money attached at the end and pass it to the fireman as the train went by. The fireman would duly shovel out the appropriate amount of coal for the eager villager to gather up.

Apart from the crowds and the associated hazards, another characteristic of the trains which I had to adapt to was their tendency not to run on time. On arriving at Madhupur, I would make my way to the announcement board. 'RT' (Right Time) against the number of your train was an occasion for rejoicing. Otherwise it might be running any number of hours late but the worst was when it ominously said 'no news'.

Once I got stranded at Jasidih station on my way back from Deoghar because of late running trains and boarded a goods train that seemed to be going in the right direction. A little further on it stopped and in the darkness I heard a familiar voice. It was the Roman Catholic priest, Father Zimoot, from the Madhupur mission and his companion. He came and joined me in the goods van but not without a great deal of pulling and pushing as he was a large man, there was no platform at that point and the lower end of the wagon door was closed. It was not a very dignified entrance. When we set off again it was impossible to make conversation above the loud rattling of the wagons.

You could hear the distant train in Fatepur, especially at night. The sound of the running carriages and the engine's whistle carried for miles over the still and quiet countryside. The villagers had no watches and those who planned to catch the train to Madhupur on its return from Giridih knew they must start walking when they heard it pass in the distance.

6

Animals—Friendly and Otherwise

The various animals that were a part of life in the village have provided me with some of my most pleasurable, my saddest and my most frightening memories.

The majority of the dogs in the village have no particular owner and survive on scraps given by the villagers and even on excrement. The male dogs fare best while the females, worn out by bearing and suckling puppies, are often pitifully thin. Some Santhal households do keep a pet dog—a throwback, perhaps, to their days as huntsmen—but more for the purposes of security now. On the positive side, the dogs have their freedom and can wander at will with no danger from traffic because there isn't any.

I couldn't help comparing these permanently hungry creatures with the pampered pets elsewhere who enjoy special dog food, 'treats', collars and grooming parlours. In spite of their rather miserable life—or because of it—the dogs I knew in the village were the most faithful and gentle companions. One would think that the scarcity of food and the struggle for survival would make them aggressive and quarrelsome but quite the opposite was the case. They nearly always waited with the utmost patience for any food. Their resigned acceptance of their fate seemed to mirror the accepting attitude of the villagers.

When I first arrived in Titmoh there was a black puppy

and a little grey kitten who were the best of friends and who played and slept, curled up, together. They were both delightful characters. The kitten, Runa, was in a miserable state. Her skin and fur were in a very bad condition and she was very thin. I think she may have been taken from her mother too soon and regarded the puppy as Mum. By the time I returned, after a few weeks absence, she was transformed. She had learnt to catch mice, rats, lizards and insects, and this addition to her diet of rice had improved her health immensely. I must say I didn't always appreciate the sound of crunching bones under my bed at night, or the tail I found in the morning. Later, when she was older, she perfected the art of catching bats in flight. She was quite a talkative cat and didn't just miaow for food, but in appreciation and greeting too, or just to answer when spoken to.

The puppy's mother was Tiggery, the first of several generations of her family that I got to know during my years in the village. She was not a particularly good-looking dog. She was light brown, of medium size with pointed ears. She had the sweetest temperament. Worn out by puppy-bearing, she was not an extrovert but she was an affectionate and intelligent creature. When I started to go out into the villages on my own I could hardly speak the language; I was unfamiliar with the surroundings and consequently greatly lacking in confidence. Tiggery appointed herself my guide and companion. She came everywhere with me and was a great source of comfort. I knew she would always find her way home and, somehow, just having her with me made me feel less of a stranger.

A young man was once brought to me, carried on a bed, in a very serious condition. He was severely emaciated and anaemic, and he had been coughing so much he couldn't speak. I diagnosed TB and commenced medication. At the time, this involved taking tablets, and being given injections twice a week. However, the day his next injection was due, only his mother turned up. She explained that she was unable to find someone willing to carry her son to the centre. I decided that once I had finished seeing the other patients I would go back with her to her home and give the injection there. I had never been to her village before and hadn't realized how far it was. We walked for several miles. Tiggery, of course, came with us though she would wander off at tangents as dogs do. The first part of our walk was across a wide, open area with extended views in all directions, and then the path dipped down into a village leading us past beautifully made Santhal houses and magnificent tamarind trees. I did not know this at the time but it was beside one of these trees that I was later going to live.

We eventually came to a stream and beyond it to another village and then to the jungle. Her village of Nayadih was in the jungle. She was a widow and obviously very poor—her home was a little one-room mud hut with a leaking thatched roof, badly in need of repair. (When the roof of a mud hut leaks, once the rains start, it doesn't take long for the walls and floor to begin to wash away.) Her son, Sahoot, was lying inside in the darkness. I gave the injection. Sahoot's mother said she would take me back to Titmoh but I felt this would be too much for her and pointed to the dog. I must say that when I refused Sahoot's mother's kind offer, it was more from concern for her than from any great confidence in Tiggery. But once we turned to make the return journey, Tiggery set off purposefully along the same path that we had come. She was going at a spanking trot and determined to keep up, I started running after her. It must have been rather a comical sight—memsahib running after a dog through the jungle! The worry was not so much about getting lost but that if I did, I would lose time and darkness would fall. Eventually I called to her and was relieved that she stopped for me to catch up. After this she trotted on and, every now and again, would stop and look behind to make sure I was still there. She led me home safely.

Sahoot's mother would come to collect her son's medicines. She had managed to arrange for someone to give him the injections at home. Some weeks later a young man came to see me. He looked slightly familiar. It took me a few minutes to realize that this was the same man who had been brought to me on a bed. He had put on weight and his face had filled out. He was smiling shyly and he had brought me an armful of maize.

One day I was very distressed to find that Tiggery was ill. She was lying up against a wall and was reluctant to move. I carried her into my room and tried to feed her and give her something to drink, but with little success. She lay there for a couple of days. During this time Runa had some kittens in a corner of my room. Tiggery somehow managed to stagger up to go and see them. She stood there swaying unsteadily and wagging her tail. It was touching to see what pleasure it gave her to see them although she was so ill.

The following day I went to Madhupur to talk to a doctor about some patients and, as I knew this doctor liked dogs, I told him about Tiggery. He tended to be rather a prophet of doom and told me it could be rabies. I assured him that I didn't think it was because Tiggery showed no signs of aggression. Then, much to my alarm, he explained that there was also a 'dumb', paralytic form of rabies and, as he described the symptoms, they did seem to fit. I realized I had unwittingly exposed myself to the risk of infection by trying to feed Tiggery and getting her saliva on my hand. Although the risk was slight, one couldn't take any chances as the illness is always fatal. He advised me to go to Calcutta to get anti-rabies injections.

It was not a pleasant experience making my way from

my Calcutta hotel to the Pasteur Institute each day for two weeks and joining the two hundred or so other unfortunates to be injected with a serum that, in those days, was a toxic mixture made out of sheep's brains. However, I was lucky to be among those to whom this treatment was available. I later learnt that the wife of a friend of ours in Jagdishpur had died of rabies.

In the meantime poor Tiggery had to be tied up as a precaution. It became all too apparent that she had rabies and she suffered terribly. Being in Calcutta, I was spared the pain of seeing her suffer. It was a horrible and tragic end for such a lovely dog.

Tiggery had had many offspring and passed on to them her docility and intelligence. She had a daughter, Pongo, ugly and neglected but with a most affectionate and selfless nature. I once saw to my amazement that this small, skinny dog, who had hardly the strength to suckle her own pups, was quite happily suckling a kid goat.

Blackie was Pongo's son. It was surprising that such a small, ungainly and timid dog should produce such a big, handsome and confident son. For Blackie, or 'Master' as Manan called him, grew up to be a very striking animal indeed and became something of a legend in the area. He attached himself to me. Although I had tried to maintain a degree of detachment, I came to feel a certain responsibility for Blackie and actually put a collar on him. He followed me over the fields to the station just as his predecessors had. I used to distract him when the train arrived by throwing him some bread to eat. Once I was catching the evening train and it was getting dark. I threw Blackie some food and managed to get on the train quickly when his back was turned. It was about half an hour's journey to Madhupur. Having reached the little house where I stayed when I was in town, I made myself some supper and went to bed. It must have been after ten when I heard a sudden rattling and scraping at the door. I went to open it and there, to my amazement, was Blackie, very excited and pleased with himself. It crossed my mind whether he had waited and come on the next train! After that I would keep him with me and take him on buses and trains if I could. This was not always easy when the buses or trains were crowded. I remember one journey by bus where both of us were standing precariously on the step at the door. I was holding on to the rail with one hand and Blackie's collar with the other. He was very cooperative and took it all in his stride—which couldn't always be said of the other passengers! Of course it wasn't possible to take him when I was going further afield. I would ask someone to try and keep him in the village while I left surreptitiously. But he would always follow in the end. Bochi, Mr O' Rourke's cook, was convinced that Blackie travelled to and fro by train. Sometimes when I enquired if he had seen Blackie, he would reply, quite seriously, in Hindi: 'He arrived by the 9.15', or 'He left by the 11.30'.

My most extraordinary memory of Blackie is of the time when he met us on the railway platform after a long absence. Manan and I had been away in England for more than two months. As we stepped off the Calcutta train at Madhupur, who should be there at the precise place where we alighted but Blackie! He was ecstatic. He danced around us with joy, knocking over our bags and making his funny, deep baying sound. It was amusing to see the surprised expressions of the other passengers as they watched this display. At first I assumed he had come with one of the villagers, but no, he was on his own. Whether it was pure coincidence, or something like the villagers making preparations for our arrival that had made him realize we were coming, I shall never know.

Unfortunately Blackie got the wanderlust and began to disappear for days at a time. He would suddenly reappear one day with a great show of affection. Sometimes he came back with his once sleek, shiny coat in a dreadful condition, and I would do my best to treat it—and then he would go off again. One day he disappeared and never came back. Maybe the lure of life outside the villages had proved too much.

Runa, the cat, had long since disappeared. There had been an awful noise of animals fighting one evening and it had been difficult to identify the terrifying sounds. We went out cautiously with torches but couldn't find anything. We never saw Runa again after that evening and I think she may have been killed by a snake.

I have always had a terror of snakes. Fairly soon one develops the life-saving habit—as it turned out—of never putting one's hands or feet anywhere without looking first. That means always shining a torch on the floor before you step out of bed at night. The villagers don't usually possess a torch, so they tap a large stick on the ground in front of them to frighten away the snakes when they walk about in the dark. The tap-tap of a stick approaching and receding as a villager passes by at night became a familiar sound. I had developed snake-awareness to such a degree by the time I came back to England that I jumped when I came out of the back door one day and saw the hosepipe lying on the ground.

It was several months after my arrival that I had my first encounter with one, and I was let in gently. It was during the daytime and the snake was fairly small and thin. Since the cat was playing with it I assumed it was not poisonous.

One thing I discovered about snakes was that they usually turn up when you least expect it. I was going about my business inside the house when I noticed that someone had put the rope we used for pulling water out of the well under one of the beds. I thought this was an odd place to put it and was about to pick it up when I saw it move. It was in fact a common krait which, along with the cobra, is one of the deadliest snakes. I met another of these creatures in front of the house one evening when I was going out to check on a patient. I called to our neighbour across to come and deal with it, but unfortunately his eyesight was not very good and he couldn't see it. So there ensued an amusing conversation in which a feeble-sighted villager tried to assure an increasingly distraught English girl that there was no snake, while she tried to assure him that there was.

The worst time for snakes, I learnt, was the monsoon, especially after a downpour. It was with this in mind, and consequently in some fearfulness, that I set off one evening to Jagdishpur in the moonlight with a group of Indian visitors from the city. The rain had now eased off and the pale moonlight was sufficient for us to follow the white, winding path without much difficulty, but it was not enough to see clearly anything that might be lurking on it. My Indian friends spent the whole journey grumbling at me for shining the torch as it hampered their night-vision, and ridiculing the idea that we might come across a snake. So it was with some satisfaction that I found one lying right across our path as we approached Jagdishpur. For once I had expected it.

My most memorable encounter with a snake was, once again, during the monsoon and I was alone in the house. The rats were often very troublesome at night and this particular night they seemed to be having a party. I got so fed up with the noise that I got out from under my mosquito net to try and restore some peace and quiet. I do not count rats amongst my most favourite animals though I do have some admiration for their abilities. It is unfortunate that those abilities often seem to be of a destructive nature and that they are not very discriminating about what they use to line a nest with. I have lost various items of underwear in this way and, on one occasion, a bold rat was seen coming down from the rafters, making its way swiftly to the table, snatching an airletter which had just been written and was lying ready to be mailed, and making off with it back into the roof. The thing about the disturbance they make at night is not just the noise but the worry. You lie in the darkness listening to the banging and clattering, and wonder just which of your possessions they have turned their attention to. They are very shrewd creatures—as soon as you shine a light they freeze and everything goes quiet as if it was all your imagination. No sooner than you turn the light off and the racket starts up again.

On this occasion, I soon gave up and was going back to bed when, as I did so, I realized that the noise was actually coming from the front and not the back room. For some reason, I decided not to investigate any further. The next morning I busied myself putting away some medicines and sorting out a trunk full of medical equipment. It was the time of the year when frogs came into the house and congregated in damp corners such as behind the trunk. I pulled it out to expel the frogs and saw an enormous cobra there. I didn't stay to examine it in detail and made a very hasty and vocal exit. There were only some women and children around at the time. One old woman, who seemed quite fearless, went in and sat down right in front of it. Eventually other villagers were rallied but they had some trouble killing it. I couldn't help feeling sorry for it. It was probably the noise of the snake eating the frogs that had disturbed me in the night. My guardian angel must have stopped me from investigating in the darkness.

7

The Disappearing Forest

Years ago, the area where we were living was covered by dense forest where wild animals roamed including tigers. There were few people then. A hundred years ago there was still thick forest and even within living memory, much of the forest had survived. Older villagers would relate how they had lived on wild fruit and berries in times of hardship. The season of greatest hunger, the hot, dry summer months, is the season of ripening fruit—mangoes, belua, banyan fruit, plum, custard apple. The forest also provided firewood, timber, medicine prepared from leaves, roots and bark, and shade from the scorching sun. The Santhals set off on their traditional hunt each winter with bows and arrows. But there is hardly any game left to hunt now apart from the odd rabbit or two and small wild fowl.

Now the forest is all but gone. The areas that the villagers refer to as 'jungle' are not what we imagine by the term. Many of the trees there are no more than stunted shrubs. During our ten years in the village many of the remaining beautiful trees, standing here and there in the fields, were chopped down. I believe it is illegal to cut down a mahua tree but this made no difference. The landscape changed before our eyes, the views extending further and further towards the horizon.

The soil is sandy and, exposed to the fierce sun and wind

in the dry season and violent storms in the monsoon, it suffers from erosion. Paths change course as, year by year, the land beside them is eaten away to form deep gullies. In some places deposits of sand and rocks even threaten cultivation in the paddy fields. The women are obliged to walk further and further afield in search of firewood. When I first arrived wood was still used for cooking but now in many villages dried cakes of precious cow dung, which could otherwise be used as manure for the fields, is burnt as fuel.

One of the most prominent trees of the forest is the sal (*Shorea robusta*). These large, semi-deciduous trees could be found over wide areas across north India. They do not grow to a great size in this region but a sal tree with a girth of 6.4 metres has been recorded in the north-eastern state of Tripura! The sal is important for its timber. It was used extensively for making railway sleepers and telegraph poles. However, the villagers told us, it was mainly because of its use as props in the coal mines that the depletion of their forest had begun.

It is sal leaves that were collected by the women to make into leaf plates. Another product of the 'jungle' from which some women made a meagre living was datwan twigs sold as disposable toothbrushes. This latter practice was far more detrimental to the regrowth of the forest than the picking of leaves.

Besides the sal, the mahua tree (*Bassia latifolia*) was common in this area. With its gnarled trunk and clusters of leathery oval leaves, it is slow to mature and its timber is very strong. It is used for building roofs and doors. The succulent, pale-yellow flowers it sheds at the beginning of the hot season turn brown when dried and are distilled to make liquor or eaten as a vegetable. They used to be so plentiful that they had no market value. Now they are expensive and quite hard to come by. The mahua played a central part in the lives of the Santhals. The liquor made from its flowers is an important part of their culture and festivals. The fruit of the mahua, round and green, is rich in oil. The oil was extracted locally and used both for cooking and applying to the skin. Now the widespread incidence of vitamin A deficiency (to which lack of oil in the diet contributes) is evidence of its scarcity.

Of the fruit trees, mango, jackfruit, custard apple, papaya, plum, bael and guava are the most common. Bael is a large, round, pale-green fruit with a very hard shell and orange pulp. It is very useful in the treatment of dysentery. Jackfruit can grow to an immense size and weight and is highly regarded as it fills the tummy and is a saleable item. Sometimes it is stolen from the trees. Often the fruit would be picked before it was ripe and cooked. There were also some magnificent tamarind trees with their long pods of sour fruit used for flavouring and chutney. The wind passing through the tamarind tree next to the health centre sounded like the sea. The children used to fearlessly climb it to a great height by pulling down the end of a lower branch and manoeuvring along it upside down to the centre of the tree and then upwards. Neem trees, of which there were a few, are renowned for the medicinal and antiseptic qualities of their bitter-tasting leaves. The banyan tree opposite the health centre was wide enough to provide shade to a large number of assembled villagers. Its fruit is eaten by humans and animals alike.

As the forest dwindles many aspects of the peoples' lives are threatened—social, economic, cultural. Eventually their very existence will come under threat. Their poverty is one of the main reasons for the deforestation and they are caught in a vicious cycle. Lack of resources forces them to sell trees and the loss of trees in turn contributes to their poverty and decline. In times of crisis and need because of an illness, a bad harvest, a wedding or death feast, a tree might be sold in order to raise cash. A tree that is sold is inevitably cut down, either because the timber is needed or simply to avoid any future dispute over ownership when the land it is growing on belongs to the vendor.

In recent years the regularization and implementation of ownership law has caused an acceleration in tree felling. In the past, ownership of a tree had accrued to the villager whose family had traditionally gathered the fruit of that particular tree. Now, by law, trees belong to the owner of the land they are growing on. This has led to serious disputes, in some cases even resulting in murder.

But the villagers' poverty and their connivance in deforestation is only part of the story. Large areas of land belong to the government and some parts are designated 'reserve forest'. Deforestation has been taking place at a disastrous rate on these lands too. In fact, it is not unusual to find that some 'reserve forest' is no more than a desert of barren, rocky land with not a tree in sight. Illegal felling by contractors and others who, presumably, bribe forestry officials, is commonplace. It is carried out quite openly and it is no secret that certain local communities, who have little land or opportunity for honest employment, earn their livelihood in this way. Thus corruption and poverty go hand in hand in destroying what remains of the forest.

The villagers are well aware of the degradation of their natural environment. To some extent, they consider deforestation as a natural process and not something they are responsible for. Planting a few fruit trees near their house is a normal thing to do, but planting a large number of trees in wasteland is not something they are accustomed to. Doing so would involve a big change in attitude, especially when there is no economic benefit in the short run and they are absorbed in the struggle to survive from day to day. It is difficult for them to spend time today on something that will only bring benefit in years to come. The produce of trees are not considered an essential part of the diet but more as a luxury, and the concept of fuel as a commodity is lacking. In the same way as water is 'free', a given provided by nature, so too, no doubt, they consider fuel as 'free'—not something requiring payment or something in return. Apart from these attitudes there is the very real practical difficulty of protecting young trees from the goats. For tree lovers they are a real menace.

Our own efforts to encourage tree planting came up against all these problems. At one time we embarked upon a programme which combined the building of an earthen dam with planting trees. The area lay between two villages on a badly eroded slope. The paddy fields lying below were threatened year after year by the deposits of sand brought down from the completely barren land above which was officially designated as 'reserve forest' belonging to the Bihar Forest Department. It was only a matter of time before the villages themselves would be threatened. It was here that we planned to plant trees in order to stem the erosion, save the paddy fields and prevent the silting up of the dam. The site of the dam was a narrow gully (formed by erosion) with rocky soil on either side. It needed to be filled in and then the whole bank raised. The water collected could be used to water the trees in the early stages and, later, to irrigate the paddy fields.

Manan went to the forest department in Deoghar to obtain permission for the project. His reception was cool and unhelpful. Sometime later the district forest officer (DFO) appeared in the village but did not come to speak to us. He was probably not sure how to react to this unusual situation. He was loath to give permission for work to take place on government land, to plant trees in a 'forest'! But he was also nervous about stopping it.

There was much work to be done—designing and budgeting for the dam, digging the pits for the saplings and organizing the workforce. We paid men and women the same rate which was very unusual. The employment was welcome. At the beginning, before the onset of the monsoon and the start of work in the paddy fields, many villagers participated including pregnant women. One woman started work again only ten days after giving birth. Generally, it was the men who hacked out the earth and the women carried it to the dam in baskets on their heads.

We decided to encourage the villagers to collect seeds and raise the saplings themselves which we would then buy from them. We provided them with the plastic tubing to do this. Our aim was to grow about one hundred mahua trees and two hundred sal trees. Protecting the trees was going to be the big problem. Rather than spending money on protection we wanted to focus our efforts on motivating the villagers to look after them and to keep their animals under control. To this end we had meetings and discussions with the villagers. One of the ideas that came up was to plant shrubs that were unpalatable to goats. I would go to the children in the fields where they were looking after the animals with pictures I had painted showing them the different ways in which trees benefit us. One of them represented villagers embracing a tree while the tree embraced them with its branches!

Work continued on the dam during our absence in the summer and was overseen by an intelligent young Santhal called Dula who was a former patient of ours from a distant village. He kept neat records. The raising of the saplings was overseen by Lutan, who was from a village near the dam. During this time we wrote an article for an international journal called *Environmental Conservation* which included photos of reserve forest and sent a copy to Dr Qasim, Secretary of the Department of Environment in Delhi. No doubt as a result of this publicity and the intervention of Dr Qasim, who subsequently wrote to the Bihar government, we received a visit, shortly after our return, from the now chastened DFO. He explained that he had not responded to us earlier due to a shortage of funds. We pointed out that we had merely been seeking permission not funds.

Apart from the saplings that were raised by the villagers and by Lutan in particular, we went by bicycle to distant plantations beyond the district boundary to dig up and bring back seedlings of acacia and sal that had seeded themselves under the trees. Lutan, who had become very enthusiastic, was thrilled to find so many seedlings when we reached there Later, he went there with fellow villagers and came back with hundreds more. Their idea was to bring a great many, of which a few might survive, while ours was to transplant a few carefully with soil around the roots. Our method was obviously more cumbersome.

There are always a few individuals like Lutan who depart from the general trend. Somra, one of our health workers, was another. He had planted some jackfruit trees near his home. When I saw them I felt like laughing. They were well and truly protected with branches and brambles about a metre deep all round!

The homegrown seedlings were distributed ten per household. We were not very impressed with how some of the villagers planted them and wished we had given better instructions. They tended to plant them like paddy seedlings, pushing them into the ground, and did not fill the earth in around them well. We had mistakenly assumed they would know how to do it. However, we were fortunate in that after the planting it rained for the first time in days.

It was heartening to see in the next few days that some of the villagers cared for their trees and filled up the pits with topsoil and manure. Sometimes when I went to visit in the evening I would find some villagers watering their trees. But we were very unlucky with the weather. Due to the drought that year 80 per cent of the trees eventually died. Not only did the trees lack water, but the villagers were more preoccupied than ever with their own survival.

However, as a result of our activities and the publicity generated, the forest department began an extensive replanting programme. Unfortunately the only trees they planted were fast-growing acacia and eucalyptus, or, as the villagers called them, 'alcasha' and 'liptis'. No doubt they helped to stem the erosion and, for a time, created employment in the digging of pits and trenches. But they were of little direct benefit or interest to the villagers. I doubt if they were intended to be.

Some years later, when we had established the health centre in Fatepur, the villagers collected seeds from many of the traditional trees of the area that were becoming quite rare, including some used by the Santhals for medicinal purposes. We planted them and tended to them in an enclosure beside the health centre. When the trench dug around the area proved inadequate in keeping the goats out, we put woven bamboo protection around each tree and fenced the enclosure. Every now and then a cry would go up that goats were eating the trees again. It was particularly bad after the paddy had been harvested and the animals were left to wander more freely again. It caused a certain amount of friction. One particular villager whose goat was a persistent offender said they had agreed to us building a health centre but not to planting trees! But others were as angry as we were. Eventually, in desperation, we invested in brickwork around some of the trees. It taught us how hard it is to keep the saplings alive. I hope it taught the villagers that it is worth the effort. For now, several years on, there is a wonderful orchard full of spectacular specimens of a wide variety of local trees—mahua, mango, tamarind, neem, polash (otherwise known as 'flame of the forest' as in March it is covered with orange flowers), date palm, bael, bohira, gamar (which is used to make musical instruments such as the violin), banhata (which has thick seed-pods over eighteen inches long), argun, sisu (a birch-like tree), plum, custard apple and popro. The exclusion of goats has allowed the grass to grow tall and we have seen birds there that we had never seen before.

8

Surviving from Harvest to Harvest

The winter months in north India are surprisingly cold, especially at night. As soon as the sun goes down at about 5 p.m., the temperature drops dramatically. A lingering warmth emanates from the blackened seat around a Santhal house but there is a distinct chill in the air until the sun rises next day. Without adequate clothing, the villagers suffer from the cold. Their skin becomes dry and cracked. Scabies is common at this time of the year as washing in cold water is less inviting. This is also the season for coughs and colds and burns. Old sarees are stitched together in layers to make bed quilts, the saree border carefully used to decorate the edges. The glowing embers of the fire are mixed with dry cow dung and rice husk, and placed in an earthen pot under a rope bed to provide some warmth. The villagers seldom drink tea but savour the hot rice-water, *mar*, which is poured from the cooking pot and mixed with a pinch of salt. Early in the morning and in the evening little improvised fires are lit outside with twigs and dry leaves, and groups of villagers huddle around them to fend off the gnawing cold. But the days are warm and bright, and food is more plentiful.

For now the paddy harvest is in full swing. It is a busy time of the year. The paddy is harvested by hand and carried to the threshing floors to be beaten in bundles against a sloping stone. The paddy falls to the ground and later this beaten paddy straw is spread over the threshing floor for the bullocks to trample out every last grain. The paddy straw is then twisted into long ropes. One person stands at one end twisting the rope while another person feeds in more straw at the other end. Finally the rope is coiled around an inner lining of straw into which the paddy is poured. The containers stand about four feet high and are so tightly packed that they are said to be rat-proof.

Apart from having their own rice to eat at this time of the year, some villagers who have managed to fence off an area against goats and have a water source nearby have grown vegetables: aubergine, tomato, onion, potato, bhindi (okra), radish and beans. Some also grow a kind of dal which does not require irrigation and gets sufficient moisture from dew.

For the Santhals the annual hunt with bows and arrows takes place at this time though it is now more of a tradition and a social event than an occasion for feasting. Coinciding with the harvest, a huge mela is organized a few miles away at Burhai. Relatives come to stay with those who live nearby and thousands converge on the big, black rock beside the Patro river. They walk, cycle and come in jeeps and buses, stirring up the dust as they pass. Many animals are sacrificed. There are sweet stalls, trinket stalls, amusement stalls and lotteries. The main Santhal festival of Bandanah takes place over a few days in the month of January with much dancing, singing and drinking. The women, decked in their best sarees, their shining, oiled black hair adorned with flowers, link arms in a row and dance from one end of the village to the other, while the men beat drums and play their flutes, and the children run excitedly alongside.

By the end of February the weather is beginning to warm up. The mahua flowers are ripening and will fall mainly at night towards the end of March. Those lucky villagers who still own mahua trees set off at dawn with baskets to gather them. The succulent yellow flowers are distilled to make liquor. Now the few small plots of wheat along the stream and beside irrigation wells are also ready to be harvested. When it rains during this time of the year, the villagers take advantage of the moist soil to plough their land.

As the days become a little longer and the heat intensifies, the time for cultivation is over. But custard apples, mangoes, jackfruit, tamarind and papaya fruits will soon be ripening on the trees. Often these are picked and eaten before they are ripe.

For many, the store of paddy is already dwindling. Now it is vital to earn money to buy food. Men who have sought employment outside in the coal mines of West Bengal or as labourers in town have already left the village. Stone-cutting is taking place nearby and both men and women work there. It is back-breaking work. While the men break up the rocks with hammers, the women load the pieces on to the trucks. They are taken to the stone-crushing mills in Jagdishpur to be made into road chippings. Sometimes a better-off villager employs others for land-levelling to prepare new paddy fields. But many families subsist entirely on the proceeds of leaf-plate making. From the picking of the leaves to the selling of the plates, a great deal of labour is involved for very little reward. The women go each day with their bamboo baskets to collect *sakua* leaves from several miles away. Later in the day the plates are made, spread out to dry, gathered in, pressed, counted, tied into packs of twenty, and then bound into long, heavy bundles. These are carried several miles to town about twice a week to be sold to middlemen. Some women leave in the evening and catch a train to another town to sell the plates at a slightly higher rate, returning early in the morning. There seems to be a tacit agreement that they will travel ticketless but every now and then there is a clampdown.

At the height of the hot season another type of leaf picking takes place—the picking of *kendu* leaves. The women brave the fierce heat and hot winds to pick these leaves and deliver them to the contractor in counted bundles at various collection points. These leaves are made into bidis (small cigarettes). The rate per thousand leaves is an issue of contention every year and is always very low. The hot season is also the season for arranging weddings. These are occasions of both celebration and hardship. They entail great expense in terms of the presents which need to be purchased, the food for the many guests and the loss of earnings from time spent not working. In many cases the villagers have to resort to taking a loan from the moneylender by mortaging their land. At this time the trains and buses are full to bursting as marriage parties criss-cross the countryside. Hindi film music over loudspeakers breaks the silence of the night.

Now resources are stretched to breaking point. The animals become thinner as the land turns brown. The number of TB patients increases as lack of food reduces resistance. The *loo* or hot wind starts as early as nine in the morning and only gradually dies out at dusk. It sucks all moisture in its path so that you are not aware that you were sweating until you step inside away from the wind and then suddenly the sweat pours off you. The wind spreads dust everywhere.

When the first rains come in mid-June there is great relief—relief at the respite from the heat and relief at the prospect of another harvest and employment in the fields. Children splash and play happily in puddles and streams. After a downpour the temperature becomes bearable for a while. It may rain for days at a time or there may be long gaps in the rain. Sometimes the rain comes very violently; you can see the threatening, reddish-black clouds gathering on the horizon. Then the fierce wind and rain tear away branches and roofs. The mud walls start to disintegrate and collapse, and courtyards become muddy. Roofs leak and frogs proliferate, congregating in damp, dark corners of the house. This is the time when the snakes come out. It is also the time of the year when the number of patients suffering from diarrhoea increases as water sources are more prone to contamination.

After heavy rains getting about becomes difficult, the dried-up streams that were easy to cross before become raging torrents. Paddy fields fill with water and the bandhs between them become slippery and treacherous. Paths turn into streams. Almost before your eyes the land turns green and the animals can eat more plentifully again and grow fatter.

Work in the fields starts in earnest. Many villagers are not able to cultivate their land themselves. They may have mortgaged it to a moneylender or they may not have bullocks to plough it, or paddy seed to sow, or they may not be able to afford to pay the labour—in cash or in food—to help with the task of transplanting and harvesting. They might overcome some of these problems by hiring bullocks or taking a loan of seed. If not, they would give the land to someone else to cultivate in exchange for half of the harvest. Those who are not working on their land hire out their labour in exchange for two meals a day and a few rupees.

The cow dung the villagers have been collecting in pits has already been spread on the fields. When the rains commence the fields are ploughed and the paddy seed is sown in the nurseries. These are situated in the lower fields which collect the most water. It takes about a month for the seeds to grow into seedlings. Then the fields are levelled by bullocks dragging a heavy wooden board. The scene is now set for the laborious job of transplanting the paddy seedlings into the waterlogged fields. The seedlings are carried to the fields where the women plant them. Standing all day in water and bending down to push the young plants into the ground, often in the pouring rain, must surely be a test of endurance. However, the camaraderie of working together and knowing that you will have a full stomach at the end of the day help to make it bearable.

The success of the paddy harvest depends on the rain. There are no facilities to irrigate the paddy fields. When the rains fail—which doesn't simply mean that there is not enough rain but that the gaps in the rain are too long and the fields start to dry out—the paddy begins to die. The upland paddy dries up and dies first. As the paddy dies so too do the villagers' hopes for the year to come. The repercussions are great—hunger, more disease due to lower resistance, more theft, more trees cut down and more soil erosion, more families broken up as men leave to find work outside. The moneylenders increase their stranglehold.

Those who have grown a little maize harvest it in September. For those who are able to grow it, the maize crop is a welcome staple food, coming as it does before the paddy is harvested.

The rains lessen and the paddy ripens in the fields. As the monsoon comes to an end a busy period of repairing houses, walls and courtyards begins. There are threshing floors to be made too, by levelling an area of ground and smoothing it over with a layer of mud followed by a layer of diluted cow dung which dries hard in the sun.

As one surveys the peaceful countryside under the clear blue sky, and watches the children laughing and playing, it is hard to imagine there are dramas and struggles for survival taking place here every day.

II

THE STRUGGLE FOR HEALTH

9

Health Care in the Village

We considered the health care project we were engaged in as a means to an end rather than an end in itself. Had we seen it as an end in itself we would have concentrated our efforts on setting up a small hospital, building up its resources and facilities, and establishing a more formal medical training programme. No doubt there was a need for such an institution but this is not the direction we wished to take. Such places already existed in other areas—islands of excellence in a sea of poverty. They brought short-term benefits for some but did not bring change.

We considered our health work as a way of coming closer to the villagers and establishing a role for ourselves whereby we could help them bring about improvements in their lives. A concern for people's health inevitably takes one into their lives—the way they live, the food they eat, their customs and values. We did not want to set ourselves apart from them and simply provide a service to them. The idea was to be involved in their lives and for them in turn to be directly involved with the work we were doing.

Underlying our work was the conviction that the problems faced by the poor villagers tended to be common to them all and could be effectively overcome only when they came together and organized themselves to challenge those who exploited and oppressed them—moneylenders, quacks, corrupt officials and politicians. Clearly, though, the health work was important in its own right too. Proper medical care was non-existent in the villages. Our work showed them the benefits of health care that they were not used to receiving and made them conscious of their right to receive the benefits.

Many of the diseases they suffered from were preventable. Poor diet, in particular the lack of protein and vitamins, and contaminated water were a major cause of ill health. As was the failure to take proper care in the initial stages of an illness and the lack of hygiene when attending to cuts and wounds. Although many diseases were preventable, that is not necessarily to say that it lay in the hands of individuals to prevent them. While each individual is responsible for his or her own health as far as circumstances permit, it is wrong to put the onus for healthy living on the individual. Prevention of disease is a social, economic and political responsibility; it has to be a collective endeavour. We did not engage a great deal in health education as such, or 'health promotion' as it is called nowadays (in recognition perhaps of the fact that ignorance often plays only a limited part in ill health). In so far as we did engage in it, it went hand in hand with treatment. When people are ill they require treatment, care and support. When receiving it they are more likely to listen to advice on prevention.

Practices that are unfamiliar to us may appear to indicate ignorance on part of those who follow them. But sometimes this judgement reflects our own failure to see them in their social, cultural or economic context. Traditional customs, seemingly unsophisticated and unresearched, can turn out to be superior to our own apparently more 'scientific' and 'advanced' practices. For instance, squatting in childbirth is now considered a good practice, and massage is recognized for its healing qualities and stimulation of the body's defence mechanisms.

It is a mistake to assume that people in villages don't know about nutrition and hygiene. They may not know terms like 'carbohydrates' and 'vitamins' but most traditional diets are 'balanced' and the villagers' diet of rice, vegetables and lentils, with some meat occasionally, is very healthy—the problem is that many villagers can't afford it. They may not know about germs but they are well aware of the need for cleanliness. However, often, they cannot afford soap or a change of clothing, and the cold in winter is not conducive to a daily bath. Ironically, there is more danger from newer customs coming from outside such as bottle-feeding of babies and consuming polished rice. In many ways their way of life is a great deal healthier than ours—no traffic pollution, no electromagnetic radiation, no high sugar and fat intake, no pesticide residues or lack of exercise!

Often their failure to take prompt action and proper care of a sick person made the situation worse than it might have been. Why did they wait so long before seeking treatment? This happened even amongst those who lived nearby and could easily come to us for treatment. Obviously it wasn't just the difficulty of getting treatment or the cost of it. It could be very frustrating and made us feel that we cared more than they did. It had to do with habit and a high degree of tolerance of discomfort and ill health. So, for example, scabies was one of life's small problems that was tolerated—until it resulted in nasty, infected wounds. Their apparent lack of care represented a different value system in which a degree of discomfort was considered a normal part of life. Once they had decided they needed treatment, however, they sought it straightaway, sometimes in the middle of the night!

Our facilities were limited. We had a small dispensary, mainly comprising essential generic drugs and basic equipment which included intravenous infusions, nasogastric tubes, catheters, suturing material and plaster of Paris. We had a microscope and carried out blood, stool and sputum examinations and ESR tests. Manan performed some minor surgery—removing foreign bodies, suturing and lancing abscesses. Occasionally he reduced fractures and did so without the aid of X-ray and anaesthetic. In this age of modern medicine and dependence on technology this may be considered crude and primitive. Our training encourages us to follow certain strict lines of procedure from which we should not deviate. Yet for centuries, till relatively recently, fractures have been reduced successfully without the use or risk of X-rays. With good clinical skills and careful examination you can feel a fracture and the position of the bones; you do not need to see them on an X-ray. Sedation and analgesia help a little, and the involvement of the patient who has confidence in the doctor can go a long way in increasing the patient's pain threshold while the bones are being realigned and stabilized.

With rapid advances in diagnostic medical technology, there is danger of a corresponding decline in the clinical skills of doctors and of lowering their confidence in their clinical judgement, something very necessary and useful in the villages. Ultrasound scanning in pregnancy is now considered a routine necessity, yet how many babies, even in difficult situations, were successfully delivered by skilled midwives before it was invented!

Sometimes we were obliged to improvise in ways that might have been frowned upon in more sophisticated circles. On one occasion Manan managed to remove a stone lodged deep in a child's ear. He did so by directing a loop of silk suture thread through the tube of the auroscope (meant for examining the ears) in such a way as to slide it into a tiny space at the side of the stone and thus hook it out. Necessity is the mother of invention.

The portable solar-powered lamp we eventually acquired

was invaluable. It was plugged into the solar panel on the roof during the day and then unplugged and switched on in the evening, giving us at least five hours of light. It was a great help when we had to deal with emergencies at night for which we had previously been dependent on torch light.

In general we aimed to recoup the cost of our medicines but did not, of course, charge for our time. Our medicines were bought in bulk from a non-profit organization and so were available at a fraction of the price they were available for in Madhupur. We did subsidize the cost of treatment for TB as it was simply not realistic in most cases for our patients to bear the full cost. Also, when a patient died we rarely had the heart to ask the family for payment. We ourselves were fortunate to receive a small living allowance from Quaker Peace and Service, based in London.

At one time we introduced a system of health cards whereby each family paid one rupee a month. The idea was that this money would go towards the village health workers' monthly allowance and help make the project self-sufficient. Those who came from a distance and would not be able to make regular payments had the option of paying a five-rupee fee per visit instead. Unfortunately the system proved difficult to sustain because it was not possible to refuse treatment to a patient who did not have sufficient funds or to those who had fallen behind with their payments. And it was too time-consuming to follow up on arrears.

Of course, sometimes we were faced with patients we were not able to treat. If possible we took them or arranged for them to be taken to an appropriate place where they could be seen by a gynaecologist or an eye surgeon or whoever the situation called for. On a few occasions, with great difficulty we took seriously ill patients to centres with more facilities than we had where we felt that their chances of survival would be higher. They invariably died. We came to realize—

as indeed I have often been reminded during my nursing career—that it is not just the equipment and the facilities you have at your disposal that determines the outcome of a case. The quality of care is equally important; the sort of care which observes closely, reacts promptly and helps build the patient's confidence. No amount of technology can make up for lack of care. Taking a patient away from familiar surroundings can also have an adverse effect on his or her condition and chances of recovery. We eventually decided not to transfer very sick patients. It was better to do all we could ourselves: if they died at least we had tried our best.

I was once relating to a doctor in the town about a sad case in which a patient had been brought to us at the last moment and had died. He said, 'You should be careful or the villagers will turn against you.' I was puzzled. Nothing could have been further from the truth. In a strange way, we seemed to come closer to the villagers when one of them died. When we cured someone we were imbued, in their minds, with a power that separated us. When treatment wasn't successful we faced suffering and death together.

The vast majority of doctors do not want to live or work in the villages. They belong to the upper classes of society and aspire, on the whole, to a high and comfortable standard of living such as is possible only in urban settings. Their training has accustomed them to rely on machinery and laboratory tests. For the most part their aim is to earn money and there isn't much of that in the villages. The absence of medical care in the rural areas and the unscrupulous activities of quacks pointed to the urgent need to train village health workers.

The role of the village health worker is generally associated with the delivery of primary health care—the dispensing of simple remedies for common complaints, the administration of immunization and imparting of advice. This is indeed very useful and can be life-saving. It can be achieved fairly simply by teaching the recognition of certain signs and symptoms and the appropriate drug for treatment so that the village health worker will know how to give, for example, iron tablets for anaemia and paracetamol for a fever.

The decision whether or not to teach village health workers to give injections became a controversial, and in some ways symbolic, issue. Many in the medical profession did not consider it necessary or appropriate for village health workers to administer injections. It was as if this was somehow the preserve of the medical profession and crossing this line would mean the encouragement of quackery and a challenge to its monopoly. Interestingly nowadays this debate is mirrored by one involving the respective roles of doctors and nurses. In response to the increasing workload of doctors in the West, nurses are seeing their roles enhanced. Greater emphasis is being given to individual accountability and responsibility rather than to the traditionally rigid demarcation of duties.

We took the view that village health workers should be taught to give injections. This was based on the principle that we should not put constraints on their learning and that they should be capable of responding to situations that might require injections. We wanted to empower them as much as possible by providing them with the relevant knowledge and skill. It made more sense that they should learn to give injections and put up drips safely than be prevented—probably unsuccessfully—from performing such procedures. We looked upon their training as a continuing process and aimed to make it as comprehensive as possible. In an ideal situation, with facilities to refer and transport seriously ill patients to a doctor or a hospital, it would not be necessary to develop the medical role of the village health worker beyond that of providing simple remedies, first aid and advice.

However, often the situation is such that there is no one else to turn to for help.

Teaching villagers who have had little or no formal education is a challenging experience. It requires a close knowledge of the trainees and their background and an ability to explain in a clear, imaginative way so that they remember things. We wanted them to comprehend and grasp, not merely learn parrot-fashion. They had to be capable of making their own judgements based on their knowledge rather than merely follow instructions. They had to develop the ability to question and criticize. It was, of course, a slow process that required constant revision and reinforcing, and an ability on our part to reconsider our own assumptions. We learnt not to assume that a picture or illustration would necessarily make our meaning clearer. Once I showed them a picture illustrating how contamination of stream water can occur and was dismayed to find that they thought the stream was a snake!

The health workers learnt a great deal on the job working with us on clinic days. While we wanted them to be capable and efficient in their medical work, we did not want them just to be 'little doctors'. We saw their role as encompassing more than the treatment of disease or giving specific advice on health matters. So, apart from learning about anatomy and physiology, pathology and the types of diseases they were likely to encounter, including psychiatric illness, we tried to put their work in its social and political context. We discussed issues related to drug companies, the prescribing habits of doctors, quackery and so on.

We wanted to make them aware that the roots of ill health often lay in the people's social and economic conditions, which in turn depended on their political environment. Symptoms of cough and emaciation could indicate the presence of TB bacilli, but also indicated a society in which the poor lived in a state of chronic malnourishment and were denied the basic preconditions of a healthy life. So treatment did not just mean eliminating the TB bacilli; it also meant helping to build a more just and equitable society. Combating the activities of the moneylenders and corrupt government officials, and encouraging the planting of trees were as much part of their job as administering medicine. In this sense their role was quite different from that of a doctor who tends to treat patients in isolation from their environment. Our hope was that as ordinary villagers themselves, they would be able to identify with the poorest and most vulnerable sections of society, and help to bring greater awareness and unity amongst them. It was not easy. We were conscious of the constant temptation faced by the health workers to model themselves on the traditional concept of a medical worker—someone who earned a good deal of money and was raised above his fellow villagers. For some this temptation was too great and they could not continue to work with us. But those who gained the conviction that their own economic betterment was, ultimately, inseparable from and dependent on the betterment of their community, were able to work with a different kind of spirit and commitment. They understood that health care should be measured not by the number of patients successfully treated but by the degree to which the people are in control of the conditions and means to lead a healthier life.

10

The Tetanus Patient

One day, not long after my arrival at Titmoh, a patient was brought to me on a bullock cart. He was squatting hunched up in it, supported by his brother. It must have been an awful journey. It was the peak of the monsoon season and it had been raining solidly for three days. The visit was unexpected and the cause of his complaint was at first a puzzle to me. The few villagers who could afford a bullock cart would usually go elsewhere for treatment—to the local quack or to a doctor in town. Perhaps it was the unusual nature of his illness that brought them to me, or my successful treatment of another patient in their village which was some distance away.

His relatives explained that he had difficulty eating and drinking. Even as they were talking and I began examining him, he was seized by a sudden, severe spasm. His brother held his head until it passed. Then I noticed that he had a very nasty swollen and infected wound on his thumb. Could this be tetanus? I had never seen a case of tetanus, only read about it. I left them for a few minutes to consult a book. From what they had told me about the wound and the onset of symptoms, it seemed likely that it was, but what could I do? I prepared a long-acting injection of penicillin and gave it to him to help control the infection in his thumb and then sent them away. It seemed very inadequate but it was all I could do and I tried to comfort myself that even with greater facilities his chances of survival were slim.

The next day I had planned to go to Madhupur. It was a tiring five-mile walk from Titmoh to Jagdishpur station over the sodden, slippery fields in the continuing rain. When the train reached town, I went to purchase some medicines from the chemist shop. As I stood at the counter, I remembered the tetanus patient and asked, feeling rather foolish because it seemed like a silly question, if they had any anti-tetanus serum. To my amazement they had some and brought out a vial to show me. I held it in my hand, looking at it and wondered what to do. It was very expensive. Maybe the man had already died. I was not sure where his village was and how I would get there to give it to him. Somehow these considerations did not seem sufficient reason not to try and save a man's life. So I went to Choudhary, my shopkeeper friend, and he agreed to lend me some money. I then went to see the block medical officer. He welcomed me in his usual friendly way. He had worked in England and liked to talk about it. He wrote FRCS after his name but I was not sure how authentic the letters were. I explained about the patient and my need for a jeep to take me to him. He was not at all enthusiastic. But as I spoke to him he gradually came round to the idea, more out of a sense of adventure, I think, than any particular desire to help a villager. He eventually agreed, though still with some reluctance. I went away to buy the serum and do some other shopping, saying I would return by three.

As I walked back up the hill to his residence loaded with my shopping, I saw his compounder and driver pushing the jeep. My heart sank. It seemed that we would not be able to go after all. The doctor explained that the jeep was out of order but they were working on it. I sat and waited in his dingy surgery. I decided that if it was still not working by 3.30 p.m., I would give up and catch the train back to Titmoh.

At precisely 3.30 p.m. they managed to get the jeep going. We set off with the doctor driving and his compounder in the back. It was still raining. At Jagdishpur we stopped at a teashop to ask the way to Karipahari, our destination. Becoming frustrated with the teashop customers' attempts to give directions, the doctor persuaded one of them to accompany us in the jeep. He obediently climbed into the back of the jeep. About three miles further on we turned off the metalled road on to a track. It was difficult to make out where the track was, as a large part of the area was under water.

From time to time I plied the doctor with some sweets I had with me in an effort to keep up his spirits though I was rapidly coming to the conclusion that we had embarked on a foolhardy expedition. Trying to save someone's life did not feel at all like a heroic business but in fact a rather miserable one. The rain continued to pour down and made the going extremely difficult, not least because visibility was so poor. Our guide turned out to be not much of a help. Presumably he was more used to accomplishing the journey on foot on small paths and through paddy fields than in a jeep. After some time we spied a shadowy figure through the rain. The doctor prevailed upon him also to join us in the back of the jeep. We continued slowly on our way. Every now and again the doctor would stop the jeep and the compounder would jump out of the back to reconnoitre. The poor fellow was getting soaked to the skin. We eventually found our path blocked by a field full of water. The jeep could go no further. We sat there looking blankly at the scene ahead of us. It would be getting dark very soon. We didn't have much idea about how much further we had to go. By now I was feeling quite guilty for landing us all in this predicament and didn't dare make any suggestions about what we should do. I gave the doctor another sweet. I looked at my watch and tried to calculate how much daylight was left. Then, after several minutes, all at once, the doctor dramatically decided that as we had come this far we should continue and he got out of the jeep. He quoted something to me in Bengali to give support for his decision.

Our feet sank into the wet ground but we set off as quickly as we could. We seemed to be walking for miles. As each house came in sight I became hopeful that we were reaching our destination but our guide would continue past. This happened again and again, and I was beginning to feel desperate. At last we came to a house where, to my relief, he went inside. The patient was still alive, squatting in the dark interior of the house. Normally certain precautions are taken when giving an intravenous injection such as sterilizing the needle and giving the injection slowly. These precautions went out of the window. As the doctor gave the injection I began to wonder if all our effort was only going to hasten our patient's demise. Our visit lasted only a few minutes. We did not linger but set off quickly on our return journey and it was dark by the time we got back to the jeep.

The doctor began to express a childish delight at our success exclaiming, 'We did it! We did it!' and put his arm around me which made me feel distinctly uncomfortable. I did not share his sense of triumph. And our troubles were not over yet. Due to a momentary lack of concentration—it must have been because the track was not too bad at this point—the doctor steered us off the track and the jeep landed at an angle of forty-five degrees, its wheels stuck deep in the wet, sandy soil. The long-suffering and very wet compounder bounded out of the back of the jeep once more and energetically set about freeing the wheels. I was beginning to wonder if we were destined to spend a large part of the night there but fortunately the compounder's efforts were rewarded and we were soon back on the track. It was with a sense of great relief that we arrived back on the main road.

The doctor tried to persuade me to come back and spend the night at his place but I had no intention of doing so. I insisted that he put me down at Jagdishpur although I had no idea how I would get home. He put me down with some ill-humour and told me, quite seriously I think, as a doctor would to a nurse in the ward, that the patient should have another injection tomorrow.

Jagdishpur was dark and wet. I did not have a torch. All the teashops had closed for the day and there was hardly anyone around. After some time I managed to find someone and asked to borrow a torch. They led me to one of the closed teashops with a slit of light still showing through a gap in the shutters. The occupants were not happy about memsahib going back alone and two young lads were found to accompany me. The trek back by the dim light of the torch—in the unrelenting rain, up and down slippery embankments, through rushing streams, over raised bandhs with water-filled paddy fields on either side, through sleeping villages where dogs started barking—seemed very long indeed. It had been a tiring day.

I was too exhausted to go back next day. But I did go back on foot later. It was about a two-hour walk. The village had a different aspect in the light of day, under a clearer sky. It was up on a wooded hillside above a meandering stream and is one of the most picturesque villages in the area. I gave the patient another injection and dressed his wound. Gradually the spasms lessened and he could eat again. He must have been immensely strong. I found out that he worked in the coal mines in Bengal. He had come home for the planting season. So they were quite well-off compared to the other villagers. They did not repay me for the injections but they did give me some eggs.

I never met him again. A few years later I heard he had been killed in a mining accident.

11

Sekirna

I first met Sekirna soon after I arrived in Titmoh. She was a Muslim and lived in the village of Durgapur about five miles away. She had a very swollen abdomen and looked for all the world as if she was pregnant. It was a cruel irony for she explained to me that her husband had left her sometime back because she had failed to produce a child, and she was living with her mother. I was at a loss as to what I could do to help her. But she was very persistent and came to see me several times. Eventually I arranged for her to be admitted into the government hospital in Giridih. This was my first experience of a government hospital in Bihar. The conditions in the hospital left something to be desired. The list of drugs I was given to buy at the chemist's, which included antibiotics and anti-tetanus vaccine, did not inspire confidence in their standards of hygiene. However, the lack of facilities and cleanliness was made up for, to some extent, by the friendliness and sympathy of the lady surgeon who had agreed to operate. She removed a tumour weighing about five kg. There was considerable anxiety about Sekirna's condition during the operation but she pulled through. I was surprised to learn that she had been diagnosed with abdominal TB at the time of the operation and so I commenced treatment for TB.

Of course Sekirna was immensely relieved to have her tummy back to normal size. After that, she was a frequent visitor and always brought something for us—some vegetables or fruit she had grown, or some cakes she had made. Once she invited me for a meal but at the last minute I was unable to go, as I had to look after a very ill patient. I felt bad not being able to let her know, imagining how she would have made a special meal and I had let her down. But she arrived later in the afternoon bringing the meal with her, neatly wrapped up, saying that she knew that something must have kept me back. I was touched by her faith in me.

I think that in spite of her position of a deserted wife and her misfortune, she had gained a good deal of respect from her fellow villagers—the women anyway—for her independence and enterprise. She used to bring patients from her village to see me. She took pride in her appearance and was always neat and clean. Her ears were adorned with rings all the way up their lobes.

About eighteen months after her operation, Sekirna started to have some pain again and I took her to a doctor in Madhupur. He said he could feel a lump and it appeared that the tumour was growing again. Sekirna was understandably very depressed. I came to know that a lady surgeon, Dr Pradhan, happened to be living in Madhupur at the time. She had been a leading gynaecologist in Calcutta and abroad. She was a small, frail-looking woman with a lovely smile that made the top of her nose wrinkle up. She related, in a very philosophical way, some of the tragic events of her life which included the death of her only child, betrayal by her family and serious illness.

Although the two women, Sekirna and Dr Pradhan, came from different worlds, one a poor, uneducated villager, the other a highly educated and accomplished professional, they had both suffered greatly at the hands of husbands, family and because of illness. Yet both confronted their misfortune with an amazing degree of fortitude and lack of self-pity.

Dr Pradhan agreed to operate on Sekirna and was able to use the facilities of Kodai Hospital to do so. She refused to take any money. While operating she discovered that what the surgeon in Giridih had diagnosed as TB had in fact been malignant deposits. Sekirna had cancer and should have had her ovaries removed at the time of her first operation. Dr Pradhan told me Sekirna would need radiotherapy in two or three months' time. I had no idea how or where I would arrange radiotherapy for her and I was about to leave the village for several months. I began to question, rightly or wrongly, how much time and energy I could spend for one patient at the expense of my other work.

But she wasn't just a patient now, she was a friend. When, after a long absence in England, I returned to the village, I took her with me to Calcutta to the Chittaranjan Cancer Hospital. Of course she had never been to Calcutta before and the fact that she agreed to go showed her courage and determination to get better. Calcutta was exciting and daunting for her. In the hospital she was examined by some doctors who recommended another operation but it was too late to register her that day and we returned the next morning. We waited several hours to find out if there was a bed for her. We went again the following day and waited again with a crowd of other patients for more than four hours. It was the resident surgeon who made the decision about allocating free beds. I asked if I could see him personally. They took me to him. He was sitting back in his chair smoking a cigarette and, without a word, he wrote 'regret' again on Sekirna's paper. He asked me to leave but I stayed. I started speaking in Hindi upon which he showed a little more interest and told me to go and see his superior. On the way down the corridor I met a pleasant lady doctor I had spoken to before and who had told me she used to know Dr Pradhan. She asked me what had happened, then took Sekirna's paper from me and went back to the resident surgeon's office. I heard an animated discussion take place for a few minutes. Whatever she said did the trick: Sekirna was in. Afterwards one of the other patients who had been waiting sidled up to ask how much I had paid. He assumed I had given a bribe.

As I could not abandon Sekirna in the hospital, the problem of finding someone to visit her and keep an eye on her now presented itself. I had been given a couple of addresses by a Quaker friend a long time ago. I made my way to one of them expecting it to be a woman but in fact it turned out to be a man! He invited me in and we talked. He said he knew the director of the cancer hospital and I should have contacted him earlier. During the course of our discussion, he mentioned someone he knew called Shomen who worked in the villages outside Calcutta. I was interested and took the phone number. After several attempts I managed to make contact. (At that time Calcutta phones were so bad that a death memorial to them had been erected by way of protest!) As luck would have it he was in town and I was invited to supper—they would send a car for me! I had grown unaccustomed to such luxuries. We had an interesting conversation but I was very tired and supper didn't arrive till eleven. Amongst other things he had been involved in wind-pump research, something I was very interested in. Three had already been set up which worked, until they were blown down that is. I didn't manage to find a visitor for Sekirna on that occasion but I learnt a little about wind pumps.

The next day I had breakfast in the hostel with a Japanese boy who had just had the rare privilege of an audience with the Dalai Lama, but had then had all his travel notes and address book stolen (such are the highs and lows of life in India it seems). I then set off to the second of my addresses. The lady in question lived in a big, old, rather dilapidated Victorian building and was having a bath when I arrived so

I sat and sipped tea in a large, dimly lit room amongst numerous cats. She was middle aged and turned out to be of a friendly disposition and we were soon engrossed in conversation. She said she would introduce me to a couple she knew who were working in a Samaritan group in Calcutta and lived in the compound of St Paul's Cathedral, the big church in Chowringhee. We arranged to meet there in the evening. These people were most welcoming and without hesitation said that they would take responsibility for Sekirna and visit her every day. They invited me to supper before which they said a little prayer for Sekirna's recovery and afterwards took me back to my hostel. My efforts to help her had brought me in contact with middle-class Indians devoted to trying to help those in need through the implementation of socialist principles and innovative technologies in one case and Christian love in the other.

I returned to Calcutta a few days later, just before Sekirna was to have her operation, and found that my new friends had indeed been very kind to her, even buying her a new saree. After visiting time, I went to see her doctor and he told me I needed to buy some blood for her. He didn't explain things very clearly and disappeared. I waited and waited. I tried to go upstairs to the ward again but the doorman at the base of the stairs stopped me. He was standing there with a bunch of keys like a jailer. Frustrated and weary, I decided to make a dash for it. I waited for an opportune moment then tore past him up the stairs as fast as I could. I had to get to the second floor and would have made it but for someone coming from the other side. The doorman had pursued me and grabbed me roughly. That was too much. I swung my umbrella at him—and collapsed in tears. A nurse came to my assistance and a crowd gathered. Sekirna was very upset. I collected the blood samples, took them to the blood bank outside the hospital, paid for the blood, bought some medicines and then returned to the hospital. In the meantime the ward master had come. I explained what had happened. He called in the doorman and berated him for taking his guard duties too literally. I quickly shook his hand by way of forgiveness and fled.

Sekirna's operation was an 'open and close'—the tumour was inoperable. The surgeon said that she did not have long to live and that he was surprised she was still so well. In fact she lived another eighteen months.

She was not happy at home and spent long periods with me in my little house in Madhupur. When she felt well enough she cooked and swept and washed. She enjoyed joining in my activities and the comings and goings; she wasn't shy with strangers or cowed by officials. She had had no education but she was very intelligent and eager to learn. I think maybe those months in the Mad Pad were the happiest in her life; I sometimes heard her singing. She had had a tragic life. Sometimes she would relate at length incidents of her past and talk about life in her village. Most of the male population there, including her two brothers, made some sort of livelihood by thieving—in particular, cutting down trees from the jungle illegally and selling timber. Her father had died of cholera when she was just beginning to crawl. Her brothers had not been good to her and her mother, under their influence much of the time, used to give away her food and belongings to them. I regretted very much that I couldn't understand her language better and all the details of the stories she told me. She was a very strong person and refused to be brought down by her poverty or her illness. She stood up for herself and, on one occasion, had enlisted the help of the village mukhia to reprimand her brothers. Even with me, she was not averse to stating her opinion and asking me for money when she needed something. In spite of all that had happened to her, she was not a sad person: she had a lovely, beaming smile and a great sense of humour.

From time to time her health deteriorated, and she would be in pain and vomit. And then she would improve and her appetite would return again. She started taking a herbal remedy called *rhanonjoot* which she had been told might cure her. I was sceptical, naturally, but had no qualms in providing it for her. I used to buy it from a herbal medicine shop in Madhupur. There was always a crowd of people at the shop. An elderly man sat surrounded by a large assortment of dried leaves, bark, seeds and twigs, and he had an enormous old book he referred to which he told me used to belong to his grandfather. The antique nature of the man and the book gave the makeshift shop a certain gravitas.

Sekirna never gave in to her illness but at the same time, I think, underneath, she knew that she was doomed. Once we were caught in a thunderstorm when she was accompanying me part of the way home from her village. I was scared of the lightning falling around us but she said she wasn't scared because she knew it was her illness that would kill her.

When her condition took a turn for the worse, my friends in Madhupur advised me to take her home. They said I shouldn't let her die with me in case the police accused me of murder in order to extract a bribe! I didn't take any notice of this crazy idea but it did seem best for her to die with her people. So, one day, when the end seemed near, I arranged for a tonga and took her home with some provisions and painkillers saying I would pay for someone to look after her. I went to see her the following day and stayed for a few hours. I would have stayed longer but a crowd of villagers gathered which made me feel awkward.

The next day, in the evening, Manan arrived in the village for the first time. We cycled over to see Sekirna in the morning. She was in a bad way and hadn't slept that night. But she was still talking and insisted we have some coffee (something she had acquired a taste for while staying with me). She expressed her gratitude to everyone who had helped and befriended her, and apologized for any mistakes she might have made. We gave her the last of the only two precious vials of morphine I had been able to buy and, within a few minutes, she was sleeping. We slipped away. When we returned we learnt that she had died without waking. We turned to make our way back down through the stream and up the other side. As we paused at the top of the slope from where you could look down on her village in one direction and over the fields and homesteads towards Titmoh in the other, I couldn't hold back the tears. I felt so bad thinking of all her suffering, her unfailing loyalty and my inability to save her. Most of the five years I had been in the village, I had known her. At that moment, her death seemed to symbolize all the failures and contradictions in my struggle to find a meaningful role in the villagers' lives. Manan did not say anything but passed me his handkerchief. After a few moments, we set off again.

You can see the little copse where she is buried from the train. Many times I have looked out of the carriage window as I passed by and wondered what we could have achieved together if she had lived.

12

Trials and Tribulations

Lack of facilities for treating patients was only one of the obstacles we faced. We also had to contend with the villagers' apathy and, on rare occasions, even hostility, and with official corruption and indifference.

Hiro was about ten years old when we first came to know him. (Births are not recorded in the village, so no one knows exactly how old they are.) He had already started working some earlier years and, like most children in the village, had never had the chance to go to school. In our evening class though, he was one of our brightest pupils and used to help others learn to read and write. He worked for Degu Singh, from one of the better-off families in the village, and was responsible for taking his animals—cows, buffaloes and goats—out to graze at six in the morning, watching over them all day and bringing them back at sunset every day of the year. So he spent the whole day in the fields with other children, sometimes sheltering under a tree from the hot sun. They all had some animals under their care. For this they earned their meals of rice and salt with, sometimes, a little vegetable curry or some lentils. Although Hiro was not starving, his diet was not adequately nutritious; his skin was dry and cracked, and he had ulcers in the corners of his mouth. We gave him some vitamin tablets but this, of course, did not treat the cause: lack of proper food.

In 1981, when we returned to the village after an absence, Hiro was dying. He was so emaciated that he was unrecognizable. He was too weak to sit up without help and was devoid of any response or emotion. Lack of nutritious food and constant work had lowered his resistance, his condition made worse by lack of care when he fell ill. It was August and Hiro's father, Budhan, was preoccupied with work in the fields. To carry him to a doctor in town would have taken up a whole day. In the meantime he called in the local quack who gave some injections, took some money and told them to stop feeding him. As Hiro's condition had deteriorated further, his father took the next and usual step of going directly to a chemist shop in Madhupur. He came back with a bottle of tonic which had cost him seven rupees. It did not help.

One day when there was no staple food in Hiro's home, his father went to exchange a pumpkin he had grown for some rice at the house where Hiro used to work. Budhan was a thin, bent, prematurely old, rather endearing man with a protruding tooth. His pumpkin was worth four rupees; for it he received only half a kilo of rice worth one and a half rupees. What is more, an argument took place between members of the household as to why he had been given the rice at all. Hiro's father showed no sign of anger; he simply shrugged and grinned when he told us about it.

We suspected that Hiro had tuberculosis. The result of his blood test (ESR) though not conclusive, indicated that it was a possibility. Examination of sputum under the microscope could have confirmed TB, but Hiro was not coughing. We needed to arrange an X-ray but Hiro was now too weak to be taken to town for this. We started TB treatment anyway.

Our main concern was to get some nourishment into him but this proved no easy matter as he refused to eat more than a few mouthfuls. We provided food but would find that his parents had not fed it to him. He could die at any time and we considered bringing him to live with us so we could feed him. We tried hard to understand what was going on in his parents' mind and realized that they had given up all hope of his survival. For them he was already dead. We had a long talk with them, explaining again the importance of proper food and assured them that, if they made an effort, he would be up and about within a month. Together, we decided on a daily diet for him where they provided rice and green vegetables and we provided lentils, wheat flour and eggs. After that, every evening, Hiro's father would come and collect a chapatti and an omelette for Hiro. Then, one evening, we heard the tap-tap of his stick approaching again in the darkness; he was coming back. Hiro wanted another chapatti. He had set off on the road to recovery.

Hiro took his medicine regularly and made no fuss about his streptomycin injections. Little over a month later, although he still only weighed fourteen kilos, he was strong enough to make the journey to Kodai Hospital in Madhupur for a chest X-ray. Manan took him to Jagdishpur on the back of his bike. Another patient we suspected of having TB, Bhikon's wife, also came along. Unfortunately Dr Das was not there that day. The X-ray technician, a supercilious young man, was in attendance. We knew that he was in the habit of taking money on the side and that when he had a poor villager alone at his mercy in the X-ray room, he would encourage them to hand over any rupee notes they might have on them. He asked Manan for the doctor's X-ray request. Since he had not written one, Manan asked the rickshaw driver for a piece of paper and wrote out a rather unorthodox X-ray request complete with his medical registration number. He handed over the scrap of paper and the fee for two X-rays, and then went back to the market leaving Bagloo, one of the health workers, behind to collect the X-rays. They arranged to meet up at the station in time to catch the afternoon train back to Jagdishpur.

When Manan met Bagloo at about 2.30 p.m. he did not have the X-rays. He had been told to collect them at 4 p.m. by which time the train would have left. Manan, Bagloo and Bhikon went back to the hospital (a distance of some two miles) by rickshaw. The technician was in his house in the hospital compound. Manan went boldly into the house. He was very angry. The technician said the X-rays were not ready and rudely told him to leave. Manan repeated that he had come for the X-rays and a fight broke out. Two other hospital employees came and joined in. Bagloo and Bhikon fled in panic. At the sound of the commotion one or two other people appeared. When the fighting ceased the technician, in a state of high excitement, ordered the hospital gate to be closed alleging that Manan had a weapon on him. Manan was quite calm by now and remained unruffled when the technician threatened him with the police. The police duly arrived and proceeded to question Manan as if he were a common criminal. They obviously did not believe he was a doctor and the question of the X-rays faded into the background as they tried to digest Manan's audacity in challenging the technician in his own house. They took him to the police station.

In the meantime Hiro and Bhikon's wife arrived back in the village. I was shocked and upset that Hiro, who was still quite weak, had had to walk the five miles back from Jagdishpur and I wondered what had happened to Manan.

Things were not going well at the police station. The fact that Manan was a Bengali did not help matters. After some time the police inspector arrived and later, summoned by Bagloo and Bhikon, our shopkeeper friend, Choudhary. They both knew Manan, knew he was a doctor and wanted to help him. However by then the First Information Report (FIR) had been filed and the local Biharis were in no mood to compromise. The discussion went on and on into the evening. Eventually an agreement was reached with the technician that if Manan made a formal apology they would withdraw the case. But Manan refused—until he had the X-rays. So Choudhary went off to the hospital with the technician to collect the X-rays which, of course, had been ready the whole time, and Manan just managed to catch the last train back to Jagdishpur.

This is rather a dramatic example of the problems we encountered in our efforts to treat TB patients. Besides being a symptom of lack of proper nutrition, the incidence of TB in a population can also be indicative of social injustice and corruption. TB is, in general, a treatable disease (though nowadays there is an increasing risk that, with the haphazard use of anti-TB drugs by doctors and patients and the consequent resistance to these drugs developed by the TB bacilli, it will not be so in the future). Yet due to the villagers' poverty on the one hand and the corruption and apathy of the government doctors on the other, the vast majority of villagers suffering from TB fail to receive proper treatment. Some came to us from many miles away, having already sought treatment unsuccessfully with various private doctors and government centres.

Not only did the patients who had TB have difficulty in receiving proper treatment, it was not uncommon for a patient to be misdiagnosed as having TB when in fact he or she was suffering from another condition. One particularly shocking example of this was a little boy, an only child, who was suffering from malnutrition after he had been stricken by whooping cough. Whooping cough is a very debilitating disease. The cough can go on for many weeks and, often because of excessive vomiting, can easily lead to malnutrition. In this case, the little boy's cough and emaciation led the doctor to diagnose TB. He did not carry out any tests to confirm his diagnosis. The little boy's father sold his only bullock to pay for medicines. The boys condition did not improve and when we did a blood test it indicated that TB was unlikely. On another occasion a man was prescribed strepto-penicillin by a doctor, combined with myambutol. Myambutol, in those days, was an expensive 'second-line' treatment which should have been kept in reserve for resistant cases of TB. He could not afford more than a few tablets. His X-ray showed no sign of TB.

Once Manan arrived and we had a doctor in the village, in theory it should have been possible for us to be recognized as a TB centre by the government and distribute the free TB medicine to which the villagers were entitled. In pursuit of this we first went to the TB hospital in Deoghar, the nearest government facility for TB treatment. We set off very early in the morning and had arrived by 8.30 a.m. but unfortunately the TB officer was 'out of station'. Rather than return to the village, we decided to continue onward to Dumka, the centre of the district at the time, to see the civil surgeon. Before leaving we tried to phone to confirm that he was there. But, predictably, the phone was out of order. At the bus stand we learnt there would be a bus at 11 a.m. But 11 a.m. came and went and there was no sign of a bus. It had been cancelled. A bus finally came at about one, and an hour and a half later we reached Dumka, making our way to the hospital. The civil surgeon was away. We spent the night near Dumka and returned next day to Deoghar. It did not take us long to realize that our journey had been in vain. The TB doctor explained that it would be necessary to undertake some training. We said we could send five health workers. His eyes lit up. He thought we were talking about five foreign nurses. When he realized we were talking about villagers he lost interest completely.

About a month later we returned to Dumka and, this

time, were able to meet the civil surgeon. He was a Santhal himself and we were hopeful of some positive action. He advised us to send him a report about our patients. We did so. Two months passed with no reply. We went to Dumka again. He explained that he had indeed received our report and the letter following it requesting a reply, but the TB doctor in Deoghar was not receiving an adequate supply of medicines.

We then extended our efforts to Patna, the capital of Bihar. We arrived at midday and went straight to the Secretariat to try to find out who the state TB officer was and where we could find him. We did not have much joy there and decided to go and see our friend, Mr Kumar. Mr Kumar tried to make several phone calls on our behalf but without much success. He did, however, manage to find out the name of someone who might be helpful, and armed with this information we returned to the Secretariat. But everyone in the health department had gone to the Sanjay Memorial football match. We did manage to elicit the names and addresses of two other people who could be helpful. We went to one of the addresses but the concerned individual was not in. The next day we made our way to the second address and made an appointment. On our return we met a TB official who said we should write again to the civil surgeon requesting him to make TB drugs available to us and to forward our application to Patna. And so we wrote a second application. After eight months we still had no reply. We should not have assumed that, as a Santhal himself, the civil surgeon would make things happen.

About a year later we renewed our efforts. We returned to Patna and this time tried to see the health commissioner. We waited nearly two hours as he was in a meeting. We were told it would be all right if we came back later. But by the time we got back, he was in another meeting. We did eventually meet a WHO doctor. At last we got a positive response.

Three months later, a TB technician from Deoghar arrived in the village and carried out some immunizations. It seemed we had received government recognition at last. Shom went to Deoghar with a list of TB patients, only to come back empty-handed. He had not taken enough information! He went again. It is a long journey; with luck one can make it back by nightfall. All he was given was a supply of thiacetazone,* the very cheapest medicine which is useless on its own and has to be taken in conjunction with other medicines. Even so we decided to carry on and Shom went each month to collect it (probably spending as much on the train fare as the cost of the medicine!), until the summer when we were away for a couple of months and he was not allowed to take it because he did not have a doctor's signature!

Like Hiro, many of the TB patients who came to us were at death's door with hardly more than skin covering their bones. It is wonderful to see such patients gradually come back to life as they undergo treatment. But one of the hardest things is to motivate them to continue their treatment for the required length of time. Once the fever and the cough have gone and the appetite returns, the tendency is to start working again as usual and stop treatment, often with fatal results. It is very satisfying to overhear, as sometimes happens, old TB patients explaining the importance of continuing their treatment to the new ones.

Due to the serious nature of the illness and the length of the treatment, we often formed a close relationship with our TB patients. The illness has a devastating effect on a family. Inability to work means no income while, at the same time, there are doctors' fees to pay, medicines to buy, X-rays to pay for and other expenses that mean selling the family's assets, mortgaging land or taking loans and getting into debt

---

* Not in use any more.

with little prospect of early repayment.

Nunulal became a close and faithful friend and an active participant in our village work. He had been fairly well off before his wife fell ill. In his search for treatment to save his wife, he had sold the family's cows and bullock cart. He was on the point of giving up when he brought her to us. His wife recovered and we formed a strong bond with them and, through them, patients started to come from his wife's village, which was many miles away. They would leave home around 4 a.m. to catch a train to Madhupur, reach there around 7 a.m. and from Madhupur catch the Jagdishpur train, finally arriving in the village around noon.

Even after the years have passed I remember many of my early TB patients well. Rameshwar Kisku, a friendly, intelligent Santhal man, was one of my first patients; Bhole Roy invited me to a lovely meal and I have a photo of him with his family. Nunulal Baskey was a lackadaisical fellow. After initial improvement, his condition started to deteriorate a good deal and I was very worried about him. This was in my early days in the village and I was as yet fairly ignorant about the state of government hospitals. I had heard about the TB hospital in Deoghar and thought it would be a good idea for him to be admitted. It was suggested to me that a letter from the block development officer might help to get him a bed. So I went to the BDO's office. He was not there but I eventually tracked him down to the other side of town. He said he needed a doctor's letter to prove that the patient had TB but fortunately accepted a prescription. Then he needed a government stamp, which was back at his office. A couple of days later armed with the BDO's letter I went to Deoghar. The journey there took four hours and I managed to see the doctor for five minutes. It was no good. Only a letter from the civil surgeon in Dumka might help. I went back to see Nunulal. He said he had changed his mind and did not want to go anywhere after all! I discovered that he thought someone had put an evil spell on him and had stopped taking his medicine as he felt it would not do any good until the spell was lifted. I managed to persuade him to take his medicine properly and his condition started to improve.

In contrast to our close relationship with many of our TB patients, our relationship with burns patients was often fraught with difficulties. Most cases of burn injuries occurred during the cold winter months, in particular children and babies whose clothing would catch fire from a careless movement or a loose garment. Treating these patients often tested our resources to the limit, not only in terms of the equipment and the time and the patience required each day in doing delicate dressings, but also in terms of maintaining the parents' confidence in us during the long, painful healing process. We did not always succeed.

On one occasion we were called to see a little boy with badly burnt arms and hands. Part of his chest and face were also burnt. It had happened three days earlier. After giving him some sedation and painkillers, we spent about four hours removing the dead skin and then cleaning and dressing the wounds. Apart from the need to check infection, we had to try to prevent contractures of the fingers and arms as the new skin grew. The fingertips of the right hand were in a particularly bad shape and it was unlikely that they could be saved. We made a splint to try and keep the fingers straight. It was a challenge for us and obviously very distressing for the child and his family. After a few days, much to our dismay and distress, the parents, probably at the instigation of the domineering grandfather, refused to let us treat him any more. An argument broke out in the village where they lived between the family and other villagers. The family removed the bandages and dressings we had so laboriously applied and put some kind of oil on the burns. We did not go there any more but we heard that both the arms became contracted and some fingers fell off. No doubt the poor child ended up with terrible scars and deformities.

Some years later we had a similar experience but on a grander scale. Lalchand was a basket-maker. He had no land, as we understood, and made his living from making baskets, winnowers and other items out of bamboo. Amongst his children was a little boy of about seven. One day his clothes caught fire and he was badly burnt on his chest, arms and hands.

We put the whole family up in the clinic room next to the health centre where we lived. At first Lalchand seemed to be a pleasant, helpful fellow. We used to give the family food and employment when we could and treated the little boy's burns each day which took a good deal of time.

After a couple of weeks they moved to another part of the village and came for dressing each day. Now that the burns had started to heal, Somra, the health worker, took over the dressing. I was surprised to learn that Lalchand had begun to say unpleasant things about us. He also said that Somra did not clean the wounds properly, and that he had tricked us and had money on him all the time. I also heard that he had stolen and sold a bicycle in his village, and this was the reason for his itinerant existence. Maybe, I now thought, this explained why things had disappeared while they were with us in a way they never had before.

One day Somra asked him twice during the morning to bring the boy for his dressing but they did not show up until Somra had gone home for lunch. I told Lalchand they would now have to wait. At this he started shouting at me, 'So you call that helping the poor?' At first I thought he was drunk. But he was not. I felt very angry and said he should be careful what he said.

When Manan returned and heard what had happened he went to see Lalchand and gave him a gruelling interrogation, asking him what he meant by 'working for the poor' and why he thought we weren't. Lalchand must have been quite shaken but, undeterred, he arranged for the local panchayat to bring a 'case' against us alleging that Manan had attacked him and, in the process, knocked out some of his teeth! He managed to find a few villagers including Rameshwar, a Santhal, to support him. Rameshwar had been a loyal friend to us but, unlike other villagers, he had expected something special for himself in exchange and may have felt aggrieved. Manan and I were so sickened by this turn of events that we seriously considered closing down the work and leaving. But finally we decided to face the situation.

The 'trial' was to take place at another village. Many villagers put on their best clothes and went off to witness the drama. The proceedings were presided over by the local Jharkhand leader and tribal chief, Likham. It so happened that Manan had previously saved his life when he had suffered a severe and terrifying bout of haemoptysis (coughing up blood) as a result of TB. However, Likham took his position of arbitrator very seriously and this was unlikely to influence his judgement in regard to a *dikoo* (outsider). The two sides gave their version of the events. Manan had made an account of everything we had provided for Lalchand and his family. It came to Rs 400 (at the time the health workers' monthly allowance was Rs 150). Likham then asked Rameshwar what time of the day it had been when Manan had struck Lalchand. Manan wondered what the reason was behind this question. Rameshwar replied that it was evening. At this Likham asked him how, in the darkness, was he able to see Lalchand's tooth fall. Rameshwar was cornered and the 'trial' was over! Lalchand was asked to touch Manan's feet by way of penance, but Manan would not allow it. It was decided we should recommence treatment. The burns had by now become infected and purulent.

It is difficult to understand Lalchand's behaviour. It was a lesson to us that the poor are not all good people (just as not all rich people are bad!) and that kindness is not always met with gratitude. Years later we learnt that Lalchand decided to turn his hand to snake-charming to earn a living. He caught a cobra and kept it in a basket. After some time he opened the basket to take it out and it promptly bit him. That was the end of Lalchand.

Once a little baby of about two months was left alone on a bed early in the morning while his parents went out to gather mahua flowers. As the day dawned and the light began to filter through the gap between the roof and the wall, the hens became restless. They began to flutter around and knocked over the kerosene lamp. The bed the baby was lying on caught fire. Fortunately, in this case, the parents were very conscientious and listened carefully to our advice. They took great care which went some way in restoring the respect I had lost on learning they had left the baby alone. The baby's burns healed well.

Once a mother's breasts were burnt when, as she was breastfeeding, her three-week-old baby made a sudden movement that upset the little open-flamed kerosene lamp she was holding. Fortunately someone snatched away the baby in time and he was unhurt. They were very sensible people but doing her dressings was not easy. I felt obliged to express the milk in order to make sure the milk ducts did not close as the burns healed. It must have been very painful for the poor woman but she bore it stoically. If a woman is unable to breastfeed, her baby is unlikely to survive. Fortunately her sister had a two-year-old child and was able to breast-feed the baby while the burns healed.

It was towards the end of the winter one year that one of the worst cases of burns came to us. She was a young girl called Ambi and she lived in a village quite a distance from Fatepur. Her saree had caught fire and about 70 per cent of her body was burnt. It is very painful to recall the suffering of that poor girl and to reconsider the merits of the actions we took. She died nearly two months after she came to us. In hindsight, maybe we should have let her die at the beginning. Maybe, on the other hand, with better care, she could have survived. We succeeded, surprisingly, in saving her at the beginning when she was in a critical state of shock. Manan managed to cut down to a deep vein in her leg to put up an infusion.

Her widowed mother (her father had died four years earlier) stayed with her. We dressed her wounds every day. It took a great deal of time and patience. The local carpenter made a frame to keep the bedclothes off her wounds and allow the air to circulate. We put a coal fire in the room to keep her warm. Some of the more superficial wounds began to heal well. Every day her mother took the soiled sheets and clothes to the stream to wash. She kept the room neat and clean, and never bothered us. For a few days Ambi had diarrhoea and it was a nightmare trying to keep her wounds clean while trying also not to move her much as it was so painful.

In spite of our efforts, Ambi lost weight until she became very emaciated and anaemic. We were unable to maintain the high level of nutrition she required. Maybe she had simply given up the will to live.

I remember sitting up on the slope above our house, when she had faded into unconsciousness and there was just a flicker of life left in her, and praying that she would live. As if by sheer will power I could hold on to that precious thing that was inexorably slipping way. But it was not to be. I felt desperately sorry for her mother. After all her hard work and care, she deserved more than that her daughter should die. In this case it was, no doubt, lack of facilities that contributed to her death, but even in a centre with much greater resources, her chances of recovery may not have been high.

13

The Power of the Quacks

Some villagers were lucky to have a lined, 'pukka' well from which to draw their water for household use or, even luckier, in recent years, to have a tube well with a hand-operated pump. However, many villagers collected their water from streams and ponds, the same streams and ponds that were used for washing clothes and for bathing and watering animals. The way to collect water from a stream was to scoop a hole in the sand at the side and to collect the water that gradually filled up from below. In this way the water may have been slightly filtered.

It is not surprising that the incidence of digestive problems and diarrhoea was high, especially during the monsoon, when contamination was greater. Death from acute diarrhoea and vomiting can be very quick. Babies and children are more vulnerable but it can also strike down a healthy young adult in a matter of a few hours if not treated. The villagers would go in panic to the quack.

Quacks were untrained and unqualified. They picked up what they knew from chemists, doctors' assistants and each other. They had no difficulty in buying medicines over the counter at the chemist shop. They 'treated' patients in order to earn as much money as possible. What they did not acquire in cash, they made up for in land and animals. Although it was no doubt in their interest for the patient to survive, their methods were unscrupulous, and with their incomplete knowledge they made many, sometimes fatal, mistakes. For example, a woman and her baby were killed when a quack injected ergometrine to hasten delivery and caused the woman's uterus to rupture. (Ergometrine is only given after delivery to cause the uterus to contract and control bleeding.) And how many have died as a result of quack-induced infection is anyone's guess. The uneducated villager was unlikely to suspect that the 'treatment' had played a part in the patient's death. For them injections and drips—the hallmark of the quack—were the best thing available. Duped by the intricacies of the procedure and the expense, they considered this to be the ultimate form of treatment even if the patient died. It was as if the needle itself was part of the treatment, not simply a means to put the medicine into the body.

The injection culture was hard to break. '*Sui laga do, theek ho jayega* (give an injection and it will get better),' was a constant refrain. In some places even 'progressive' doctors pandered to the villagers' faith in injections 'in order to gain their confidence'. We did not agree with this approach. We collected capsules and injection vials with similar labels. When confronted by the familiar exhortation for an injection we would get our visual aids out once again and patiently launch into a mini-lecture explaining the various ways of administering medicines and their respective uses and benefits. At first this lesson would leave the patient or the relative bemused and sceptical. It was a slow process.

In a place like Bihar where malpractice and corruption are so endemic, there is often, in practice, little difference between a quack and a doctor. The former lives in the village and is more likely to visit a patient at home. The latter lives and stays in town and may charge a little less. Our local quack was a Bhumiyar (by caste) called Ramdeh and he roamed the villages on his bicycle. Some quacks had earned enough to buy a motorbike. Invariably he would put up a drip under the most unhygienic conditions, give some injections and charge a great deal of money—up to ten times the value of the infusion and medicines. The cost of treatment left the family considerably worse off and, sometimes, both bereaved and in debt.

In the 1980s, oral rehydration therapy as a treatment for acute diarrhoea was extensively discussed in journals and seminars. Acute diarrhoea (as opposed to chronic dysentery and diarrhoea, which are often associated with parasites and malnutrition) results in rapid loss of body fluid and salts. Traditionally the dehydration resulting from diarrhoea was treated by an intravenous infusion. However, it was found that fluid and salts could be effectively replaced orally, without requiring recourse to the intravenous route. This method is easier as it does not have to be administered by a health professional, and is also safer and cheaper. The diarrhoea normally stops by itself, and so long as the fluid balance of the body is maintained the patient is out of danger. Only in a small minority of cases is dehydration so advanced or vomiting so severe that it is necessary to put up a drip.

Some advocate a homemade solution containing just salt and sugar in the correct proportions, arguing that you should use local ingredients rather than make the villagers dependent on packets. Homemade remedies are an attractive idea. However, in most poor households sugar is not available and this solution is probably not adequate for dealing with life-threatening situations. In the absence of the superior solution though there is no doubt that it is better than nothing.

Much lip service was paid to oral rehydration therapy by medical professionals. But, in those days it was less extensively used in practice. Habits take time to change. When intravenous therapy is available and a patient is in a serious condition, the tendency is to put up a drip. When medical professionals do this, it reinforces the perception that this is the treatment of choice.

We learnt through experience and necessity just how effective oral rehydration can be even in severe cases of dehydration. We were passing through a village on our way to Madhupur one day to catch a train to Calcutta when we were called to see an old man who was seriously ill and dehydrated. Given the opportunity there is little doubt that we would have put up a drip but, in the circumstances, this wasn't possible as it was very difficult for us to change our plans. So we advised the man's family on how to make the solution with the packets and impressed upon them the importance of persevering with it even in case of vomiting. At the time we considered that his chances of survival were slim and felt guilty about not being able to stay to look after him. However, thanks to the solution and the family's care, we found on our return that he had survived. It was experiences such as this one that reinforced our confidence in the efficacy of oral rehydration therapy.

The ideal oral solution consists of 20 gm glucose, 3.5 gm sodium chloride (common salt), 2.5 gm sodium bicarbonate (baking soda) and 1.5 gm potassium chloride dissolved in one litre of cold water. We made our own packets of these ingredients. The contents were measured out into little plastic bags which were then sealed by the flame of a candle. Each bag was then put into a bigger plastic bag along with an explanatory leaflet that we had printed. Rehydration packets were available at the chemists' but at six times the price of ours and had other unnecessary ingredients added. Our aim was to promote our packets in the villages as a potentially life-saving, cheap and safe treatment that each household should keep in readiness.

Getting a small child to take adequate quantities of the

fluid was not always easy. The child's spitting it out was not usually a problem, but it was difficult to keep disturbing a tired and weak child in order to give him or her the frequent drinks of fluid required. In these cases we would insert a tube into the stomach which allows one to give the fluid at regular intervals without disturbing the child. This is a standard practice and, if done with care, is much less hazardous and expensive than intravenous treatment. On one occasion a small baby was vomiting so persistently that oral treatment even with small amounts was not working. So Manan passed a stomach tube and attached it to a bottle containing rehydration solution hanging from a beam. The baby's mother sat up all night holding the baby while the solution dripped very slowly and continuously through the tube into the baby's stomach and by morning the baby was out of danger. Correspondence through a magazine called *Diarrhoea Dialogue* revealed that others in similar circumstances had resorted to this form of treatment although it was not in the textbooks and requires great care and close observation. On another occasion we advised a father to give his son one teaspoon of fluid every minute for five minutes, stop for five minutes and then repeat the procedure. In the morning the boy walked one mile back home with his father.

We used various methods to promote oral rehydration and to alert the villagers about the danger of quacks. One method was to put up a play in the village. The idea was sparked off by Bhola, one of the village health workers we were training, during a lesson. He got up to demonstrate in a very effective and amusing way how a moneylender prowls around outside the house where someone has died. The bereaved family will have to arrange a death feast and, in most cases, will require a loan to do so. Hence the moneylender stalking his prey. Together we developed the story of an old man and his son who worked as stone-cutters.

They return home one evening and, joined by other villagers, chat about the stone-cutting, their wages, how much the contractor earns and how the paddy is dying. The son complains he is not feeling well. They say he has worked too hard in the hot sun. The son becomes ill and they call in the witch doctor who explains what animal sacrifices need to be performed. The villagers made this scene very funny (thus demonstrating their disbelief?). Eventually the quack is called who charges Rs 500 and gives injections. The son dies and the old man has to mortgage his land and trees in order to pay Rs 1500 for the death feast and, as a result, is left destitute.

The preparations and rehearsals were at times very frustrating and at other times great fun. Kodin, the old man, apparently spent sleepless nights thinking about his role and it even affected his ploughing according to Bhola. Bhola himself became very good at explaining to the other actors how to perform their parts—and then forgot his own lines! Several hundred villagers came to see the play, some from quite far away. It was a moonlit night and they sat on the ground in front of the school building. To begin with, while everything was being made ready, there was some singing. The opening scene featured a tea stall where a moneylender (with a cushion to give him a big tummy) and his friend, the quack, meet up and have a chat. The tea stall must have been realistic, with the radio playing in the background and smoke coming out of the stove: a person from the audience wandered up to ask for some bidis! Although they had never acted before, all the actors were good and some really talented. Some members of the audience were restive and noisy, but there was a general hush when the old man appeared and cheers when he challenged the moneylender. A few wandered away before the end. It was a new experience for them and they may have expected more singing, dancing and 'escapism' rather than the depiction of their everyday life! It was the first of a number of plays we staged. One was on politicians at the time of the general election and another was the story of Shidhu Khanu and the Santhal Revolt.

Another way we promoted oral rehydration was to set up a stall at melas and village markets. We tried to stage a ten-minute play to attract attention but it was not a success amongst the moving crowds and was abandoned. We set out the packets against a backdrop of eye-catching pictures. The response varied. At first it was often the better-off villagers who bought the packets. Once Somra was in full flow when, unrecognized by him, Monohor came up to the stall. Monohor, whose very name had an ominous ring and of whom we had heard some horrifying stories, was the quack in that particular area!

Although the packets didn't exactly sell like hot cakes, our various activities definitely set in train a process which gradually helped to wean the villagers off the quacks and increase their confidence in the oral method of rehydration. A crucial element in this was the attitude and activities of the village health workers. Somra had become a very enthusiastic convert. He would cycle tirelessly on his noisy old bicycle to distant villages with a tin box full of packets and pictures, explaining his message, sometimes in Hindi and sometimes in Santhali. Once, when we returned from a summer absence, he recounted how there had been an epidemic of diarrhoea and he had made himself a bed near the door of his house to ensure that he could hear when someone called him at night. He saved many lives.

The village health workers were central to our work and the promotion of oral rehydration therapy was an important part of it. It helped to save lives in the short run and, as a tool in the struggle against exploitation by quacks and moneylenders, in the long run too.

14

The Moneylender and the Dying Child

Pradhani was a widow and very poor; she didn't have much land. She was a small, silent, rather ungainly woman with a pockmarked face. Her grandson, her daughter's little boy, had been suffering from diarrhoea for several weeks. His name was Anil and he was about five years old. He was whimpering as she squatted on the ground in the clinic cradling him in her arms. His eyes were in a bad state, half-closed and infected. Closer inspection revealed signs of severe vitamin A deficiency. His ears were also infected and discharging pus, and he had a fever. Somra had treated him earlier but the little boy had not been brought back as instructed. No doubt the family was preoccupied with work in the fields.

I was hopeful that the infection could be checked and, with care taken to feed him properly, he would make a full recovery. I looked forward to seeing him running about again. However, the odds were against him, for as he showed improvement in one complaint another one would develop. It became apparent that his kidneys were failing. Then, one morning his mouth was full of bleeding sores and he had the greatest difficulty in swallowing. He tried hard but much of the fluid came back, through his nose. We tried changing his antibiotics and giving them by injection. I sent Tikla, one of the health workers, to town to buy some more medicines.

We encouraged his mother to bring milk for him each day and I made some nourishing soup for him, but he became thinner and thinner. I explained to his parents that I held out very little hope of his survival. They said that they were very poor and couldn't afford to take him elsewhere.

I used to go and see him again last thing in the evening. I walked through the dark and silent village, pushed open the door to their courtyard carefully as one of the hinges was broken, passed their one bullock who looked at me sleepily and crossed the little courtyard to the tiny room where the whole family slept on straw spread on the ground. I had to be very careful not to step on a sleeping child as, torch in hand, I bent down through the low doorway and stepped inside, and made my way to where Anil was lying.

The suffering of a small child is particularly distressing and troubling to witness, especially when one's efforts appear to be prolonging the suffering rather than alleviating it.

One morning when I went to see Anil, a bullock cart was standing in front of the house. Anil was lying on a rope bed in the courtyard in the warm sunshine. In another corner of the courtyard sat a fat man. He was surveying several sacks of paddy stacked in front of him. He was a moneylender and had come to take away most of Pradhani's harvest. Two years earlier she had taken a loan of rice from him on the occasion of a wedding and now had to repay the loan many times over. The scene in that small courtyard that morning was nothing out of the ordinary but the sight of the fat moneylender and the dying boy side by side brought home to me the connection between the two. The connection between exploitation on the one hand and the poverty and malnutrition that contributed to Anil's death on the other. For Anil died two days later. Most probably, with so little resistance, he had developed septicaemia. In spite of the apparent hopelessness of the situation I had kept hoping for the best but I was glad his suffering had come to an end. Soon afterwards I had to go away. I didn't see Pradhani again until I was leaving. She arrived hurriedly, just in time to say goodbye. She was not a woman to show much emotion but now for the first time I saw tears in her eyes. It was difficult to know what she was thinking but, as she took my hand, it was clear that she bore me no ill will for not having been able to save her grandson. No doubt she bore the moneylender no ill will either. For her it was all in God's hands.

15

Small Family, Happy Family

During Prime Minister Indira Gandhi's Emergency rule, her son Sanjay, though unelected, became a powerful political figure. He was an impatient and callous young man, and the power he suddenly acquired seemed to have gone to his head. He proclaimed edicts like a feudal king. Overnight, rows of little stalls by the roadside in Madhupur, which had provided their owners with a livelihood, were demolished to widen the roads. However, the policy which affected me and the villagers directly was his aggressive family-planning programme. The manner in which it was carried out put the cause of family planning in India back by several years. A great deal of pressure, including the threat of withholding salaries, was put on government officials and employees to produce quotas of patients for sterilization. Many poor villagers—young and old men—fell victim to their zeal to fulfil their quotas. In a state like Bihar where corruption is rife, the scheme, which also involved small payments by way of incentive to the patients and those who brought them, was wide open to abuse. Pressure was put on me by Dr Yadav, the local medical officer, to produce patients at 'vasectomy camps'. He made it clear that he would withdraw any support for my work if I did not cooperate. At first, being well aware of the need for family planning, I was happy to oblige and spent time going round the villages, collecting the names of candidates for the operation. I reassured those who, knowing more than I did at the time, expressed their fear about the operation.

On the appointed day only two from my list actually turned up. I was disappointed but I duly accompanied them to the building in Madhupur where the operations were taking place. I was horrified by the scene that unfolded when we arrived. Town officials lounged around, chatting jovially as if presiding over some sort of jamboree, while doctors smoked and chewed paan and patients milled around in the chaos. There were no facilities to sterilize any instruments and razor blades straight from the market were being used for surgery. In the melee, for a moment I lost sight of one of my patients and was just in time to grab him back as he was being summoned into one of the operating rooms. I had no intention of being responsible for his septic wound or worse. I took them both instead to Dr Das at Kodai Hospital.

Afterwards I wrote an account of what had happened in a letter which was published in the *Illustrated Weekly of India*, and a letter of complaint to the BDO. The latter was not well received and Dr Yadav wrote a long and insulting reply accusing me of undermining the government's family-planning programme. It made me very angry. He sent one of his minions to the village to tell me that they were expecting to see me at another vasectomy camp at nearby Burhai. Needless to say I didn't go.

Then one day the son of an elderly Santhal man we knew, Budhan Murmu, came to tell us that his father was not well. Budhan was an exceptionally responsive, intelligent and active man in his sixties. His wife was a small woman of similar age who was partially blind. She was a grandmother, well past child-bearing age. Budhan told us how, a few days earlier, he had gone to Madhupur to enquire about a loan for an irrigation well when he was approached by a man who told him that food was being distributed to the poor. He went along with the man and was forced to undergo a vasectomy. Afterwards he was given some money which the man who had taken him there took from him on the pretext of counting it—and disappeared. Budhan was in a great deal of pain, his wound was grossly infected and he had a fever.

News had come to me that Dr Yadav had prepared a 'file' against me. The file apparently consisted of three or four letters from villagers claiming that I was spreading opposition to family planning. My friend Dr Das at Kodai Hospital had seen the file and expressed his anxiety about it. This was not the last time that local government officials would be making allegations against me. Dr Das borrowed a jeep (at that time he did not have one of his own) and came to see Budhan. He was shocked by what he saw and took down a statement from him in front of the village headman. He advised me that I should do nothing in case they tried to put the blame on me, and that I should go and report the matter to Dr Yadav. He identified the villagers who had apparently signed the letter against me. Only one admitted to signing something: he had been told he was signing a work application.

I went to Madhupur the next day to see Dr Yadav and, as luck would have it, a new BDO was present when we met. Dr Yadav and the BDO came to see Budhan that very afternoon with some medicines and a scrotal support. Dr Yadav said to me that if I had a grievance against him why had I not told him so directly. I replied that my grievance was not against him personally and that it was what had happened to Budhan that I was opposed to, not family planning. The next day another jeep arrived. It was the 'doctor' who had performed the operation.

For a time I went on my bicycle to see Budhan every day to change his dressing and to have a chat. He was impressed with all the visits. He was a lovely man, always eager to talk.

He used to translate my faltering Hindi into Santhali for the womenfolk who gathered around. He talked about how things had been better under British rule. He was not the only villager who told me that. I was not sure what to make of it.

After a flurry of activity, Dr Yadav seemed to have dropped the matter. But Budhan's wound was not improving. He started drinking to ease the pain in his mind and body. After an interval of several days Dr Yadav turned up again, but unfortunately Budhan was drunk at the time. In his inebriated state he became a laughing stock which made me very sad. I took him to another doctor in Madhupur who said that the wound was still very infected and it would be better to operate to clean it up. But afterwards he was still in a great deal of pain.

I wrote a letter on his behalf, seeking compensation, to the civil surgeon in Dumka (the chief medical officer for the district). About three weeks later I went to Dumka to see him. It was a long and tiring journey. The civil surgeon claimed not to have received my letter so I related the whole story to him. When I had finished he said, 'You mustn't make capital out of this.' I was completely taken aback by this response but managed to stay calm. I tried to explain that it was precisely because I was in favour of family planning that I disapproved of what was happening so strongly. I told him that episodes like Budhan's botched surgery were counter-productive to its cause and that in order to help put things right Budhan should receive compensation. I learnt afterwards from Dr Das that he had known all about the case as they had discussed it together but he was frightened to take action against his officers. After our meeting the civil surgeon must have had second thoughts. He came to see Budhan himself the following week and got him to sign some statements about what had happened. By then the wound had almost healed.

Eventually Budhan was given 20 kg of wheat seed and 40

kg of fertilizer probably by way of compensation. He never got the irrigation well he had dreamt of. His spirit had been broken. He took to drinking regularly and within a year he was dead. In spite of his age he had been one of the most responsive and forward-looking men in the village.

No doubt incidents similar to this, which must have been repeated all over the country, contributed to Indira Gandhi's resounding defeat when she eventually called a general election. Sanjay was killed in a plane crash while performing a stunt in 1981. Dr Yadav changed his tune and tried to be friendly towards me but I did not trust him.

I did not completely abandon my efforts to promote family planning but I didn't go out of my way to do so. I tried to respond to requests made to me from time to time by the women. One remarkable woman from the village of Sultanpur was determined to be sterilized. She had seven children and pestered me to arrange the operation for her. I managed to find a pleasant lady doctor in the government hospital at Giridih. Unfortunately the day we went there it turned out she was on leave. A male doctor said he would do the operation. It was difficult to refuse the offer; I would not to have to make the journey again. After some hesitation I agreed. I felt the weight of responsibility on me. The doctor invited me to be present during the operation. My patient was anaesthetized with ether which was rather unpleasant as it seemed to take a long time to take effect. The operation had not proceeded very far before the doctor's competence appeared to be in some doubt. He was having difficulty in locating the tubes. He made a bigger incision. The technician who was administering the anaesthetic began to help. At this point another doctor came into the operation theatre smoking a cigarette. He stayed on to have a chat. I was appalled but managed to curb my initial impulse to say something as I did not want to make a scene in the operation theatre. I didn't understand enough about these things to know if there was a danger of us all being blown up, but nevertheless it did not seem a good idea to be smoking in the presence of ether—and a gaping abdomen. When he eventually left I followed him out and said that I hoped he didn't think I was being rude, but would he have gone in there smoking if his wife had been on the table? He laughed and said nothing would happen. The poor lady was in a great deal of pain afterwards and I could well believe it. She did recover eventually.

The fear of family planning and the lack of appropriate means for it led, inevitably, to the practice of abortion. Occasionally women would come and ask me for '*mahinwari khulne ki davai* (medicine to restart periods)'. I would try and explain that such a medicine did not exist and that it was very dangerous to try and do anything about it themselves. Usually they had already been pregnant for some time before they came to me. Once a mother brought her young daughter in the last stages of pregnancy. It was hard to believe they could consider killing the baby. We spent a long time trying to convince them to go away from home to have the baby quietly in some other place and promised that we would try and arrange for it to be looked after. I don't know what happened but I expect they found an unscrupulous doctor without much difficulty who did what they wanted for a large sum of money.

One Santhali girl used to go to Madhupur with her friend to earn a little money by prostitution. When she became pregnant she tried to abort the foetus herself and became dangerously ill, vomiting blood. She was brought to us five days later and Manan concluded that she had managed to perforate her intestine and had peritonitis. We decided to keep her with us and monitor her progress with 'drip and suck' treatment, resting her gut by aspirating the stomach contents through a tube to keep it empty and feeding her intravenously. We gave intravenous antibiotics to check the infection. Her condition fluctuated. One night it seemed she was going to die but Manan managed to revive her. She required attention day and night. It was a hard time for us as she was quite a demanding and difficult patient, and there was so much else to do. After a few days she improved to such an extent that we felt confident the perforation was healing and she was out danger. She was drinking a little, sitting up by herself, and her pulse, blood pressure and urine were normal. She was not well enough to go home so we decided to send her to a mission hospital near Patna where she could recuperate under medical supervision and have good food. To send her there was quite an undertaking. Manan himself held the drip as her relatives carried her over the fields to the station to catch the evening train. We stayed in Madhupur that night and put her on the morning train with her father and Somra. Manan had written extensive notes for the hospital so that they could familiarize themselves with her case. But it was all to no avail: she was not given the appropriate care and we were shocked to learn that within two days of arriving there she had died.

I consider it a human right to have access to safe contraception. For a long time I was acutely aware of my own inability to provide this much-needed service apart from distributing condoms and pills. Neither of the two were very appropriate—one because of the problem of acceptance and the other because of the irregular and inadequate supplies. It seemed to me that intrauterine devices (IUDs) were probably the best method under the circumstances. However, it was a few years before I managed to receive training in this form of family planning. It took a little time for the IUDs to gain acceptance but gradually there was a snowball effect. As some women came forward and then talked to their friends it became quite popular. My village friend, Debimaya, helped.

At first she assisted me and would extract the IUDs on the few occasions that a problem developed or the woman wanted to conceive again. As her experience and confidence grew, she began to fit them herself. The programme, still run by Debimaya, is now very successful and Debimaya has a steady stream of patients, some from many miles away. They come of their own free will and need no incentive apart from the desire to have more control over their lives.

16

The Girl from Belatar

Manan had gone to Calcutta and I was on my own in the village with Sushila, our one-year-old daughter. It was the hot season. Toota, who lived nearby, had told me not to open the door to anyone who called at night unless he accompanied them.

I was awakened in the darkness by a sudden sharp rattling at the door. I could hear some voices in the quietness and recognized one of them as Toota's. My heart sank wondering what kind of emergency it might portend. It often seemed that emergencies came when I was on my own. I fumbled for the torch and got up carefully so as not to wake my sleeping baby, and went to the door. I called through it and understood that Toota had brought a man from Belatar, the next village, whose daughter was sick with diarrhoea. I asked him to come to a little high-window. By stretching up I managed to hand him some rehydration packets through it and explained to him how to use them. It was rather an unusual consultation as we could not see each other, but I felt confident I had done what was necessary. I did not think much more about it in the morning as I went about the usual routine of washing up dishes from the previous evening, preparing breakfast and attending to any callers and patients that came. Debimaya arrived to help.

Later in the morning the man came again. I explained the

importance of giving the fluid as long as the diarrhoea continued and gave him some more packets. He did not seem to be unduly anxious. In the afternoon he came again though and, on closer questioning, it seemed as if his daughter was not suffering from a simple case of diarrhoea. He told me she was running a temperature and it sounded as if I should go and see her. I was reluctant to take my little daughter there. Although heavily pregnant, Debimaya said she would come with me and help look after Sushila. So once the heat of the day started abating, we set off. The way took us down through the village and across the stream, which was not difficult to cross at that time of the year, and up the other side to the village beyond. Many of the villagers came out to see us when we arrived and we were taken in to see the young woman lying inside.

I was shocked to see how ill she was; she was in a coma with a high fever and a very weak pulse. I tried to take her blood pressure but it was not recordable. I had a panicky feeling that if I wasn't able to do something soon she would die. It was difficult to think clearly what course of action I should take. I thought of going back to fetch some more equipment and drugs and putting up a drip. And then I realized that it was not long till nightfall. Debimaya needed to go home to her young family and I didn't relish the thought of keeping Sushila with me there while I looked after the girl. Then Debimaya suggested that they take her to our place. It took some time to persuade them to do this as they were very reluctant to move her. On the way home Debimaya went to call Shom and I quickly began to get some supper for Sushila.

It was already dark by the time they arrived, carrying her on a rope bed. Now it was up to me. It is quite a wretched feeling knowing that you are not really equipped to deal with a situation and yet there are no other resources to call on. I expected Manan back early in the morning and just hoped I could keep her alive till then. I raised the end of her bed to aid her blood circulation and collected the equipment to put up a drip. It was vital to get some fluid into her and try to raise her blood pressure. This proved to be no easy matter. The collapse of her peripheral circulation, caused by dehydration, made it very difficult to find an adequate vein. The girl's father was holding the torch for me. Once or twice I managed to put the needle in the vein but by the time I attached it to the drip it had already clogged up. Meanwhile Sushila began to cry. She had obviously sensed something was wrong and would not quieten. I had to leave the girl and spend some time trying to calm her down. I felt I had not been very clever, landing myself in a situation where I was torn between my crying child and a dying woman. I began to feel rather desperate. Eventually Shom came to the rescue and took Sushila outside. He walked up and down in the courtyard with her, showing her the wonderful night sky and was able to keep her quiet for about ten minutes. Fortunately, during that time, I managed to get the drip going and could breathe a sigh of relief. At least there was some hope now. I took Sushila to bed and proceeded with the next challenge of getting her to sleep. Then I went back to my patient.

I had learnt from Manan that in very serious cases like this you don't bother yourself with the cause of the illness (was it malaria or typhoid?), you concentrate on keeping the patient alive with fluid and stimulants. I studied the box of emergency drugs and, feeling very nervous, made a selection. When I felt I had done all I could for the moment I went and lay down. But I didn't sleep. I got up now and then to check on her and change the drip bottle.

It was very early in the morning when she started talking again that I dared to think she might recover, though she wasn't out of danger yet. By then she had had three bottles of fluid but hadn't passed any urine. Feeling rather audacious, I gave her a diuretic injection in case the kidneys needed a kick-start. It worked and from then on she seemed to improve quite rapidly. By daybreak I felt confident she would survive.

In the morning they brought her baby daughter to see her. I hadn't realized she had a child and, as I looked at the little baby I thought how near she had come to being motherless. Manan didn't come back until that evening by which time she was back at home.

17

Mental Health

It is difficult to assess the extent of psychiatric illness in villages. No doubt a great deal of it is 'hidden' but, from what did come to our notice, there appeared to be a significant incidence of these illnesses, in particular of depression. When mental illness imitated or manifested itself in a physical illness, for example unconsciousness, the villagers, naturally, showed great care and concern. However, when the illness led to disruptive and strange forms of behaviour, their response was generally much less sympathetic. Then the patients could be ostracized, ridiculed or even beaten. The village health workers were not familiar with the possibility of diagnosing and treating mental illness.

After a particularly busy day I was awakened one night by a group of villagers in great distress. They had come in a group as if by their number they would convey to me the gravity of the situation and persuade me to come back with them to see their patient in spite of the lateness of the hour. It sounded as if the patient was dying. They told me she was 'cold and unconscious'. This did indeed appear to be the case as I examined her by the light of the kerosene lamp. Many anxious villagers had crowded around her bed. One woman was massaging her with oil, another was applying warmed cloths. They had shaved her head—an ominous sign. Her husband was weeping quietly. She did not respond at all to my questions. She did not even respond when I applied painful stimuli. And yet I could find nothing wrong with her. Her temperature, pulse and respiration were normal and her pupils were reacting normally to light. I began to suspect that she might be suffering from a form of hysteria and that she was not really unconscious at all. I decided to put my theory to the test and told them I was going back to fetch an injection, a plan which met with immediate approval. I returned and injected 2 ml of sterile water. Even before I had finished giving it she had swallowed, then turned her head towards me and opened her eyes. The effect was certainly dramatic, but I had misgivings about reinforcing the villagers' often misplaced faith in injections in this manner. I did not attempt to explain to the villagers that I had injected only water. I simply emphasized to the woman's husband that she needed good care and rest, and that these were as important to her as any medicine.

A neighbour of ours showed symptoms of mental illness over a longer period. She was a friendly, intelligent woman. At one time her behaviour deteriorated badly. She did not sleep for several nights and was acting strangely, not responding to other people, as if in a world of her own. The generally held view was that she had been possessed by an evil spirit. Various efforts were made to rid her of it. These included giving her dog's urine to drink and sacrificing a cockerel. A Santhal Christian gave her some holy water! None of this worked. When all this came to our notice we gave her an injection of diazepam in an effort to sedate her, but this had no effect either. The next morning a little crowd of villagers had gathered in front of her house and were deriving much amusement from the spectacle she presented. She was repeating everything she heard, including the barking of a dog. We sent everyone away and gave her some more Valium, intravenously this time. She went to sleep, only for an hour or so but enough to calm her down and bring her almost back to normal. I sat and talked to her and we gave her a meal. Later we talked some more and she told me about a dream she had had. It seemed she had fallen in love with a young boy in the village. She made me promise not to tell anyone and she described her dream to me. Next day she told me she had had the most wonderful sleep. After that she wandered in to see us quite often and I would sit and listen to her, occasionally questioning or reassuring her. She became quite demanding, though at the same time I felt honoured that she had the confidence to talk to me so freely and was pleased that it seemed to have such a therapeutic effect on her. Her problem, however, was more deep-seated than could be treated only by talking and we gave her medicines too. When she stopped taking them she deteriorated again and developed a persecution complex. Although the villagers' attitude towards her lent some justification for this, we felt nonetheless that she was probably suffering from a form of schizophrenia.

Although most of our psychiatric patients were women, including several cases of post-natal depression, we had one unusual case involving a young man. We had been away from the village for a few days and when we arrived back in Madhupur we heard that a villager had been there searching for us. It sounded as if there was a case of encephalitis or tetanus. We returned to Titmoh in the evening and found the patient, on a bed, and his family waiting for us. In our absence they had called in the quack who had charged them Rs 200 and had told them to stop feeding him for three days. The young man was not talking. Manan examined him carefully and could find nothing physically wrong except a distended bladder. When shown some nasty-looking instruments and a catheter, he eventually managed to get up and went outside to relieve himself much to his relatives' amazement! After some sedation he went to sleep but in the morning he still would not speak. Gradually, alone with him, with a combination of firmness and reassurance, Manan managed to get him to talk a little. After that breakthrough he rapidly made a full recovery. Later we heard that the quack had tried to find out from one of the health workers which injection of ours had cured him!

Physical illness is more 'visible' and more readily understood than mental illness and, in a situation where there is such obvious need for medical care for physical illnesses, it is easy to neglect the importance of mental health care. Yet, with the inevitable stress of their hard and monotonous lives, the separation of families as the husbands leave to find work, the tendency of some to escape with drink, and the decline in supportive traditions, the need for mental health care is very real. It needs to be seen as part and parcel of community health care and not just as a service available in specialized centres for the well-off or those with severe mental health problems.   -

18

Impromptu Veterinarians

It was not uncommon for us to be asked to treat animals. We felt very incompetent to do so, as our ability to make a proper diagnosis was very limited, but it was difficult to refuse. For if medical care for humans was lacking, medical care for animals was non-existent.

The importance of animals, in particular cattle, in the lives of the villagers was reflected in their anxiety when one became ill. It sometimes seemed to me that they cared more about their bullocks than their children. Once a villager called Harpal came to me because his buffalo was ill. He came very promptly and paid for the medicine immediately. Sometime earlier, a child of his had died, largely as a result of lack of care when he fell ill. He had plenty of children and could produce another one but he could not afford to buy another buffalo.

The villagers kept cows and bullocks, buffaloes, goats and chicken. The Santhals also kept pigs. I would rather call them hogs—they were small, black and whiskery with long snouts. The bullocks and cows were small, white creatures. They became pitifully thin in the dry season and put on weight again in the monsoon and winter months. The poorest villagers did not have any animals; some had only a goat or two. Buffaloes were only owned by the better off who would tend them carefully and take these slow-moving, ponderous animals down to the pond where they would wallow and their shiny black coats would be washed.

The cows produced minimal amounts of milk. In general, they were kept to produce offspring, not milk. Whenever I told the villagers about the amount of milk it was possible for a well-nourished cow to produce, they would express incredulity. Only certain castes (like Mahto) kept cows for selling milk. The milk was transported in buckets, or in converted oil tins, hanging from a pole slung over the shoulder and had straw immersed in it to prevent it from slopping over. The bullocks were most in demand as they were used to plough the fields and, for the better off, to pull a cart. They were, therefore, an essential part of life. Without them cultivation could not take place, nor could goods be easily transported. Cow dung was a precious commodity—an essential part of building, fertilizer for the fields and, more and more, fuel for cooking.

Meat was eaten only a few days each year. When entertaining a visitor, for example, chicken curry would be served. At festival time, and for weddings and death feasts, goats would be slaughtered. Only the Muslims occasionally ate beef.

Animals functioned as a sort of bank for the villagers— when in need they would sell one to raise cash. Those who kept hens would very often sell the eggs (or hatch them) rather than eat them. Sometimes hens were 'sacrificed' as part of a ritual to exorcize an evil spirit. Chicks were very vulnerable to being carried off by kites. Whenever one flew overhead, the mother hen would set up a terrific commotion and her brood would scatter and dive for cover. Unfortunately there was often one that didn't make it. I have seen a distraught mother hen fly high into the sky in a vain attempt to rescue one of her offspring. The mortality of chicks in this way was very high. Hens were also very vulnerable to disease. At one time Somra managed to raise two hundred chicks. They all died within six days.

One of my earliest encounters with the lack of veterinary care—a sick cow—prompted me to set off to Madhupur very early one morning in search of the animal husbandry officer. Chutu's cow was suffering from what appeared to be a kind of fit. It was shaking and falling about, a horrible sight. At Madhupur, it was apparent that the animal husbandry officer was not in the habit of venturing out into the villages, and it was with great difficulty that I persuaded him to come back with me by the nine o'clock train. We couldn't find a good bicycle to borrow in Jagdishpur so he had to make do with a rather cronky affair. I could not help laughing as he struggled with it muttering 'this is a very troublesome bicycle, very troublesome'. The weather was very hot too. When we arrived at Titmoh, he could not stop as the bike had no brakes, and he went sailing on past the people who had come out to greet him, coming to a halt just at the edge of the dung pit which was full of water after a recent storm. Fortunately he was a nice enough fellow and took it all in his stride. But he could not do anything for Chutu's cow. It died a few days later.

Not long after this I heard of several more cattle deaths. A local doctor told me he had had cases of human anthrax. I decided to investigate and spent four hours one afternoon cycling round the villages with Choti, a villager. We discovered that in a small area twenty cattle had died during the previous two weeks. One bullock worth Rs 2000, a really handsome beast, had died within three hours. We came across an old man whose buffalo had just fallen sick. It was a pathetic sight. He was sitting in front of it with tears silently running down his face, giving it some jungle medicine.

The next day I went to Madhupur to see the vet although I knew that he was not someone who would exert himself unduly. He said he would send someone to Dumka to bring vaccine if I paid for it but he was not hopeful there would be any. I went to see the doctor who had told me about the anthrax and looked through some old textbooks which he produced for me. He explained to me how to inject a buffalo by thrusting the needle into its hindquarters and then attaching the syringe. I prepared a leaflet to distribute to the villagers, advising each village to have separate grazing lands and explaining the necessary precautions to be taken in disposing of dead animals. Choudhary checked the Hindi for me and I took it to be printed. Although few villagers can read, those who could, read it out to the others and it gave weight to the issue. When I returned to the village it was getting dark but I wanted to go and see how the old man's sick buffalo was. Fortunately it seemed better and was eating again. But no wonder the man was worried—six animals had died in a house nearby. Just as we were about to leave, we were called to see another sick animal. I was hesitant to go—night was falling. This animal had stopped eating. Its pair had already died. A crowd gathered as we roped it and got it on the ground. Its skin was very tough! I was pretty scared to give the injection. The next morning he seemed better, eating, ruminating and very energetic. The day after this someone else came to report another sick buffalo. By the time I arrived, it was obviously at its last gasp. I told the people it was dying and it was useless to give an injection, but they insisted that I do. I think it had already taken its last breath before I injected it.

The vet had not sent anyone to see us so it seemed no vaccine was available in Dumka. The next day I took the night train to Calcutta and went to the West Bengal Veterinary College. There I met some very helpful and sympathetic vets. They explained the importance of making a correct diagnosis before vaccinating as there is another disease called HS (haemorragic septicaemia). They told me that it can be dangerous if you vaccinate against one disease when the animal is incubating the other. So I did not collect any vaccine. Instead I sent a cryptic telegram to the Department of Veterinary Services in Patna. Not surprisingly, this did not result in the action hoped for. As the monsoon lessened the epidemic began to die down.

The following year I set off to Patna to visit the Bihar Veterinary College, an impressive white building on a large campus. After I had written my name on a piece of paper, I was shown into the director's room where there were several big babus sitting importantly in their smart suits. I sat down in front of them and explained the problem briefly—about the animals dying during the previous and the current year, the inactivity of the local vets and the fact that one of them had informed me that ranikeet vaccine (for hens) was not available. The director said they could not help me and suggested I go to Bhagalpur. I told him that I had already been to Calcutta and had been advised there to come to Patna, so it was unfortunate that I should now have to go to Bhagalpur. Thereupon he gave me the name of a doctor in the institute next door. It turned out to be the Institute of Animal Health and Production. Fortunately this man was more helpful and responsive. He suggested I should put something in writing, so I asked for a piece of paper and did so there and then. It had a dramatic effect! He started ringing his bell and summoned to his presence a Dr Sen whom he asked to return with me to the village that very day! I went off with him to his office and met some other vets. He said he could not come that day but gave me another date for his visit. When, on my return I told the villagers, they were very happy.

I had some difficulty finding accommodation for Dr Sen because the chief minister and his retinue were coming to Madhupur the same day and the Raj hotel was full of 'changers' from Calcutta. Eventually I managed to book him a room in the station retiring room. I met him at the station and the party set off to Titmoh by the nine o'clock train— the vet and his 'peon' carrying his equipment, microscope and all, a visitor who happened to have arrived, myself and Blackie, the dog. I had hoped that Bhola, a health worker, and Prabhu, a village friend, would bring bicycles for us but they had not. Bagloo, another health worker, was the only one who met us at Jagdishpur. With difficulty I managed to borrow two bicycles for the vet and for myself. Bagloo walked and the peon stayed back in Jagdishpur with the luggage. I found this odd. Only a couple of villagers had come when we arrived in Titmoh but after a little while more gathered. I fetched milk to make some tea while the vet talked to them. By the time I returned he was in full flow. To my dismay I heard him talking about me not the animals. He was telling the health workers that it was not important to learn about medicines from me but to learn perseverance, courage and confidence! If I as a foreigner and a woman could go to Patna to bring him, why couldn't they? *He* obviously had a great deal to learn!

He returned to Madhupur without examining any animals or opening his bag. In due course I received a report merely stating the sporadic occurrence of a variety of diseases!

Two years later I paid another visit to the Institute of Animal Health and Production in Patna, this time with Manan. The director whom I'd met on the previous occasion had by now retired but we met some helpful people. The best solution seemed to be to buy vaccine directly from them rather than trying to get it from government officials (whose job it was to supply it free). We managed with the health workers to immunize poultry against ranikeet, a disease to which many succumbed in the winter months, and some cattle against rinderpest. Rinderpest is caused by a virus. The vaccine was live and needed to be kept on ice. Manan arrived back with some one evening and tried to leave it overnight in a fridge in Madhupur but without success. Either the shops with fridges were closed or the fridge was not working. So we had to inject it the same day. It was a chilly night, towards the end of January. Fortunately there was some moonlight. We managed to do less than fifty and came home at midnight.

Soon afterwards a new assistant to the block animal husbandry officer in Madhupur appeared in the village one day. He seemed to be the sort who did not mind doing some work and had brought a bottle of carbon tetrachloride for the treatment of liver fluke. He explained that he immunized bullocks with them standing up, so each injection took only a couple of minutes compared with our ten to fifteen. We had tried it once but the needle had bent alarmingly.

We never solved the problem of making a proper diagnosis and continued to inject sick animals with antibiotics, which sometimes worked and sometimes didn't. It felt rather like being a quack but at least we didn't charge a great deal of money.

19

Birth and Death

At first, the nearest I came to attending a birth was to arrive just after the baby had been born. I went to the house, which was nearby, with the idea of observing and learning. I found the small newborn baby lying on the wet, bloodstained earthen floor beside the placenta to which it was still attached. It was the mother's fourth child and she was crouching in a dark corner of the room. Food was being prepared, as usual, in the same room and the other children were there. I watched and waited a few minutes. Eventually I couldn't bear it any longer so I fetched a cloth to dry and wrap the baby in, and clamped and cut the cord. I held it against me in an effort to warm it up, much to the amusement of the others present. I was loath to let them bathe it straightaway as was their custom, fearing that its temperature would fall dangerously, especially as it was winter. I was relieved when they produced some hot water from the stove—presumably this is what the midwife had disappeared to prepare when I arrived.

Since then I have seen, always with some degree of alarm, other newborn babies undergo their first and very thorough bath lying in the crook of the midwife's feet as she vigorously applies soap and pours water over them. However, I came to realize the saving grace of the human incubator. After the bath the baby remains next to the mother, receiving the warmth and humidity of her body. No doubt this greatly increases its chance of survival. Unfortunately, they did not believe in putting the baby to the breast straightaway, saying there was 'no milk'. I spent a great deal of time trying to explain the benefits of colostrum (the first milk which is highly nutritious and helps the newborn baby resist infection). Some women would accept what I said and let the baby suck—again with amusement not hostility—while others would adamantly stick to their old belief. It was interesting to note that, at least, instead of colostrum they fed the baby boiled goat's milk with a spoon and somehow knew that goat's milk is more digestible for an infant than cow's milk. In practice I think the shortage of goat's milk for many families meant that the baby had one traditional feed of goat's milk and started breastfeeding soon after. Breastfeeding was universal, thank goodness. When the mother died, a baby's chances of survival were very slim indeed.

I was very impressed one day when I was visiting a sick woman with a small baby. As I was examining her, the baby began to cry. A neighbour picked up the baby and gave it her breast as if it was the most natural thing in the world. A little boy called Ramchendra lived next door. When he was about three years old, his mother gave birth again and he was ousted from the breast. This can be an important cause of infant malnutrition especially if the first baby is very young and, as is often the case, weaning doesn't take place until the child is a year old. After the birth of his sister I quite often saw Ramchendra at his grandmother's breast. I assumed this was just as a comfort, till one day I asked Mama, as we called her, and she proudly showed me a great spurt of milk! It must have been about twenty years since she had had her last child, but sucking alone had stimulated milk production.

In general the practices surrounding a birth were a mixture of the good and the bad just as they are in 'developed' societies where, to my way of thinking, the degree of interference is far too high. I had gone to the village following my midwifery training at a time when 70 per cent of births in the UK were induced and spinal anaesthesia (epidural) was very much in vogue, pushing up the incidence of forceps deliveries.

The village midwives tended to come from a particular caste and their profession was passed from mother to daughter. They looked after the mother during the birth and for five days afterwards, not only caring for the mother and the baby but doing the washing, cleaning and housework too. They were paid with rice. After the birth they would prepare a special high-calorie sweet pudding for the mother. Their main tool of pain relief during labour and, to give a feeling of well-being afterwards, was massage. All the advantages of a home delivery that we in the West are having to relearn—the familiar surroundings, the presence and support of friends and family—played their part too. The young age at which the women first gave birth and the relatively small size of the babies probably helped reduce morbidity in labour. I feel sure these factors must have contributed to the outcome for one young mother whose first baby was a breech delivery (when the buttocks or feet are delivered first). I had never delivered a breech before and was very apprehensive as I desperately tried the manoeuvres I had learnt long back. Eventually the buttocks and legs were delivered but the arms were stuck. When I managed at last to release the arms, I couldn't deliver the head. By that time the baby was trying to breathe. We succeeded in the end, and I was amazed and greatly relieved that the baby hadn't suffered damage to the nerves in her neck.

The practice of not cutting the cord till the placenta is delivered is not harmful in itself. In fact the baby can benefit by receiving any extra blood it may be denied if the cord is cut too soon. The danger—which I tried to alert the village midwives to—is that in the meantime it is not easy to look after the baby, to clear its airway and keep it warm. Most of the midwives started to cut the cord before the delivery of the placenta. Sometimes this becomes essential. Once I heard that a neighbour of ours was in labour and, although I hadn't been called as everything seemed all right, I went along to see how she was progressing. I was alarmed to find that the baby's heartbeat was very fast and she was passing meconium-stained liquor—signs of foetal distress. It was clear that the baby should be delivered as soon as possible. We put up an infusion of syntocinon to strengthen the mother's contractions and the baby was born a couple of hours later with the cord wrapped around its neck three times!

Sometimes we learnt the hard way that the villagers knew better than we did. On one occasion we diagnosed a deep transverse arrest, which meant that the baby's head was stuck and needed to be rotated. We had tried to deliver her on a bed as usual. As we felt we could do no more to help, we advised the villagers to take the woman to a hospital. She then got up off the bed to squat and the baby was born before they had time to hitch the bullocks to the cart! I became convinced that squatting is the best and most natural position to deliver a baby, at least until the head is visible. Nowadays this is scientifically accepted.

Most of the dangers the mothers and babies were exposed to stemmed more from the general lack of hygiene and poor diet than from bad practice as such. I never, for example, came across the practice I had heard about, of putting cow dung on the cord, which obviously entails the risk of infecting the baby. We had to distinguish between risky practices and those which were just different. I saw a midwife help a mother who had just given birth stand up and support herself holding on to a beam while the midwife pushed her own head into the mother's tummy—one way of expelling blood clots! In teaching the village midwives about antenatal care I put most emphasis on better nutrition, detecting and treating anaemia, and checking for signs of toxaemia (blood poisoning).

The importance of the latter was brought home to me one day at the height of the hot season. A patient was carried in the heat on a bed for several miles. She was suffering from toxaemia and was unconscious with a temperature of 106°F. I realized it was hopeless but I tried for several hours to save her. Manan was away at the time. The relatives called a 'jungli doctor' as well and I said nothing to discourage this, only asking them to try to be quiet. (Toxaemic patients are to be kept in darkened, quiet rooms.) He performed his rituals which involved, at one point, putting a small chick on her tummy, while I sedated her, put up a syntocinon drip and tried to bring down her temperature. In the evening the baby was still born with the cord around its neck. This must have delayed the birth; everything was against her. I thought then, after the birth, there might be a glimmer of hope for her, but she died soon after. The relatives did not believe that she was dead because her body was still so warm. I passed my stethoscope for them to listen to her silent heart but even then they would not believe me. It is hard to tell relatives that the patient has died and it is not made any easier when they do not believe you.

But the worst case for me was Lilmuni's. It will always be etched in my memory, as it was the most harrowing I experienced—not simply because her death was so unnecessary, but because it showed to what depths of callousness and apathy it is possible for members of the medical profession to sink. To me the death of this young woman demonstrated how doctors can become more concerned with their own reputation than the care of the sick. It highlighted the failure and injustice of a socio-political system that provides medical care only to the rich and to townspeople and denies it to poor villagers.

Lilmuni died at about nine in the morning on 7 March 1982. The struggle to save her life had started three days earlier. She had gone into labour in the morning. Having borne two children without undue difficulty, the birth of her third child seemed unlikely to cause problems. But when, by evening, the baby had not been born, it became apparent that something was wrong. Her labour pains stopped. This was nature's way of protecting the mother for if the pains had continued and the birth of the baby was obstructed, she would surely die. She lived in the village of Sonajori about two miles from Fatepur and her relatives came to call us. Unfortunately we were away and didn't get back until the evening. Manan went to see her as night fell, crossing the fields and a stream in heavy rain. He confirmed that the baby had died. As there was nothing that could be done immediately, he sedated her and passed a catheter to relieve her distended bladder and returned home with some difficulty at 1 p.m. In the morning, as her condition had become weaker, we put up an intravenous infusion. There was some uncertainty about being able to take the dead baby out safely there and so we decided that, in spite of the difficulty of carrying her, it would be better to take her to a doctor in Madhupur who had more facilities. We were confident that her condition would improve and her life be saved.

So her relatives attached ropes to each end of her wooden bed and, with the aid of a bamboo pole, carried her the six miles to Jagdishpur and from there by train to Madhupur, with me accompanying them. She was weak but her pulse had improved following the infusion, and she was quite conscious and talking. With skilled and immediate care her chances of survival were good.

Our destination was Dr Chopra, a professed Christian who had trained in the famous hospital at Vellore in south India. As he performed Caesareans and attended difficult deliveries we knew he had the expertise and instruments to do what was necessary. To my utter amazement and shock he refused to treat her. He said, 'They are Santhals, they will not pay.' I replied that if necessary I would pay. To which he said, 'I have no nurse. I can't expect my wife to help in such a case.' (Lilmuni had started to smell a little.) I pointed out that I was a nurse and more than willing to help. Then, when he couldn't say anything, he became angry and went inside, closing the door and telling us to take her away. There are some things that, looking back, I find hard to believe really happened and this is one of them. I was quite perplexed as to what to do. The relatives took charge of the situation and said we should take her to the railway hospital. I had never been there but I agreed. They carried her up and over the bridge the way we had just come. To my relief the doctor seemed pleasant and agreed to treat her. But when he saw her he suddenly changed his mind saying he didn't have the necessary instruments. He even refused to let us keep her on the veranda outside the hospital while we decided what to do next. The nurse there tried to blame the villagers for Lilmuni's condition. Is it a villager's fault she lives in a village? Is it her fault there are no medical facilities for miles around? Was it the woman's fault that labour was obstructed and the baby died?

Of the three other doctors in Madhupur we tried to contact, one was away; one, Dr Das, was about to leave for Calcutta; and one, the block medical officer, said he had no instruments. Madhupur was a town of about 40,000 population and the block headquarters of more than 500 villages and the medical officer there had no forceps or equipment to deal with an obstetric emergency!

By now it was about one in the afternoon. We took her over the bridge once more to the Catholic mission and put her bed down in the shade. I went to the chemist to buy some intravenous fluids, an infusion set and some antibiotics to keep Lilmuni alive while the search for help continued. Dr Das agreed to lend his jeep and driver, and Father Zimoot, the Roman Catholic priest, suggested we take her to Deoghar subdivisional general hospital, thirty-seven miles away. He accompanied us.

It was a nightmarish journey. Lilmuni somehow survived the terrible, bumpy ride on the floor of the back of the jeep but she was becoming delirious. I had never been to this hospital before. I was desperate to arrive. The journey seemed interminable. I had a naive belief that when we reached there things would happen and she would be all right. But when we arrived at about five, nothing did happen. We could not even find someone to help us carry her out of the jeep. I began to help and, as I did so, out of the corner of my eye, I saw the hospital compounder snigger. For him it was a comic spectacle to see a 'memsahib' trying to help a poor villager. Finally the hospital staff found a bed for Lilmuni and left me with her. I rubbed her feet, as they felt very cold. I assumed the doctors there had gone to prepare for the operation. I became impatient and went downstairs to see what was going on. To my surprise I found the doctors sitting round a table chatting. I stood there awkwardly and asked them what they were going to do. They said they would operate 'if she revived' but that she would probably die. I suggested that she was not going to revive until they operated. So, after some persuasion, one of the doctors got up self-righteously and they took her to the operation theatre at about 6.30 p.m. They succeeded in extracting the baby under general anaesthetic without difficulty—apart from a power cut—and there was little bleeding. She came out of the anaesthetic and now I felt sure that if her blood pressure could be restored and the infection checked with proper nursing care, she would survive.

But this sort of attention is not for a poor villager in a government hospital. Her blood pressure was not checked, an intravenous infusion was put up with such incompetence that she was pricked all over and when it was finally going, there was no tape to secure the needle. There was no suction to clear her throat when she was still unconscious after the anaesthetic, and there was no oxygen cylinder. Here, even the most elementary medical facilities were only for the rich and influential.

But I did not learn about what happened—or rather did not happen—that night until later, because I had made the mistake of returning to Madhupur in the jeep with the priest. I was exhausted and felt I had done all I could and, now that she was in hospital, it was awkward for me to suggest to them what to do. One of the doctors had seemed to care more than the others but actually, after I left, he did nothing. It was one of the wrong decisions I made in difficult circumstances.

I had arranged a women's meeting in the village for the next day but I decided to go back to Deoghar by the early morning train instead, although it meant that the women would be coming some distance for nothing as I could not let them know. Unfortunately the train was very delayed and the twenty-minute journey to Jasidih on the way to Deoghar took three and a half hours. When I eventually alighted from the train in Jasidih, Lilmuni's little nephew caught my arm. He told me she was dead. We stood there—the little Santhal boy and me—weeping on the crowded platform with people all around staring at us.

Lilmuni's death and all that led up to it disturbed me so much and made me so angry that I wrote about it in a journal called *Mainstream*. I concluded the article by writing, 'There are those who will say that she was bound to die or that it was God's will or that all that could be done in the circumstances was done. I do not agree. Lilmuni Manjian's death was by no means inevitable. It was the direct result of collective negligence. It was a shameful waste of a young woman's life. Even those doctors and others who wished to help were rendered ineffective and demoralized by the general indifference. Those who treated Lilmuni as less than human, in so doing became dehumanized themselves. If this story can in any way help people to care and to think about the social causes of her death, her death will not have been completely useless. These things must change and will change if enough people care and if those who care speak out and are not numbed by a feeling of helplessness or fear for their personal safety. To care does not require a particular ideology, religious or political. It means simply to recognize that we are all human beings and if we help each other we can make life better and happier for everyone.'

III

WHO CARES?

20

The Rise and Fall of Suku

Suku Murmu is a Santhal, the youngest of four brothers. His father died when he was very young, leaving his mother to raise the children in great poverty. As a boy he was one of a handful of children who went to the little village school. They would sit on the floor in the bare room, writing on their slates and repeating out loud the alphabet and numbers. Quite often the teacher didn't turn up and he would walk the two miles home again. Suku persevered and went on to attend the primary school in Jagdishpur, eventually graduating to secondary school in Madhupur. This was an unusual achievement in this area, where the vast majority of villagers are completely illiterate. It meant getting up in the dark and walking twelve miles to the school and twelve miles back. He explained to me that he wasn't afraid of walking alone in the dark because in his mind he imagined that he had already arrived. One of the masters at the school befriended him and would give him odd jobs like sweeping to do so that he could earn a few paise to buy some tiffin.

He became a frequent visitor in Titmoh, stopping off on his way home. He liked to talk about many different things, to learn and ask questions. He loved singing and telling stories; some were elaborate ones from Santhal mythology about ghosts and vampires. He had his own broken style of speaking English which somehow gave greater impact to what he was trying to say. 'Never you worry. Always you must live happy,' he used to say.

He enthusiastically helped in teaching the children who came to our night school and became involved with us in encouraging the villagers to grow small plots of wheat and hybrid maize to supplement their rice crop. However, things were not easy for him and he had problems at home as his elder brother tried to divide their land unfairly, allotting him much less than his fair share. Against his wishes at the time, his mother, fearful that his education might tempt him to leave the village, arranged his marriage to a young girl from a neighbouring village.

In June 1978 he decided to contest in the mukhia elections. The mukhia is an elected village representative, the lowest rung of the government administration. The post had always been held by a better-off villager from the upper section of society which included the quacks and the moneylenders. Although the post is an unpaid one, it is coveted as it offers great scope for siphoning off government funds allocated for village schemes and for charging villagers for services rendered. The old mukhia had a nice two-storey brick house with a lined well. For Suku, it offered the opportunity to become the first tribal mukhia and to serve his fellow villagers.

During the election campaign, he had a band of loyal supporters and they were constantly on the move from village to village, 'moving like army', he said, on their bicycles. Their bicycles were in very bad condition, so I gave some money to pay for repairs. Some villagers, used to receiving bribes in exchange for votes, tried to elicit bribes from Suku. He became very troubled, saying, 'I am doing this for the people not for myself, why do they give me so much trouble?' 'If they said, "please friend will you give me a bidi,"' Suku would say, 'I would willingly give them one.' In the days preceding the election they worked tirelessly, hardly stopping to eat or sleep.

One night we all had a meal together at midnight and then they set about writing out copies of the lists of the two thousand voters' names and they were off again at 4 a.m.

The opposition tried all sorts of means to defeat him—spreading malicious rumours about him, applying to the authorities in Deoghar for his candidature to be rejected, providing meals for hundreds of villagers and distributing *choora* (flat-rice). We heard that altogether nineteen candidates were murdered in Bihar during the election campaign and a report said that over one thousand people had died in clashes between different groups and the police. When I expressed concern for Suku's safety, he brushed it aside saying, 'Never you worry, completely you don't worry. I am strong.'

The day of the election came. There were six other candidates, each identified on the voting paper by a symbol—a bird, a chair, a flower and so on. Suku's symbol was a woman's face. In the morning his confidence was high but it came crashing down when we heard that an officer inside one of the voting booths had been covering up Suku's symbol. The old mukhia was apparently paying his supporters five rupees to vote more than once. Although each voter had his or her hand stained with a mark when they went in to vote, some managed to vote several times. (In Jagdishpur there was one Santhali candidate but apparently at least 200 Santhals were prevented from voting by the Muslims.) When voting finished we waited in a big crowd outside the school room. A man arrived from another booth and was immediately swallowed up by the crowd eager for news. Suku had come third there. Soon after that we had news that he had won easily in Titmoh. We dashed off to the third booth and met others coming towards us halfway. Then we knew that he had won, and there was great excitement and jubilation. The total number of votes cast had been 900, much more than for the general election and Suku had won by 180 votes.

We were thrilled. It seemed like a victory for democracy over corruption and for the poor over the moneylenders. Later in the evening when his many well-wishers had left, the responsibility and opportunity of his new position began to sink in and he told me about one village he had been to when he was canvassing where he found the people living in particularly wretched conditions. 'So difficult I feel,' he said. Now he was happy he might find the means to help them. He said, 'The people are living blind. They must open their eyes so that others can't suck their juice any more.'

The reality was, though we didn't see it then, that by becoming mukhia, Suku himself had joined the ranks of the juice-suckers. He had become a part of a system based on bribery and corruption, and his 'downfall' was inevitable.

For a little while after the election the ousted mukhia continued to make threats against Suku. Once I went to Madhupur with him. I returned from Jagdishpur by bicycle in a thunderstorm and he set off on foot with a friend. Night fell and he didn't arrive. A search party set out to look for him with the usual bows and arrows, axes and dogs. They found him involved in trying to solve a dispute in another village. He came to spend most of his time dealing with disputes of various kinds and was overwhelmed with advice and demands from all sides. He told me he sometimes felt he was going mad and needed to go into the jungle to be alone. I tried my best to help him and suggested that he leave dispute-solving to the sarpanch (deputy mukhia). When I brought him a harmonium from Calcutta he was very happy and, when he had the chance, he would sit and compose songs. In September 1978 his wife gave birth to a little girl and they named her after me, Jan.

Over the course of time I saw less and less of him. But I heard about him from the villagers and was saddened by what I heard. I would not say that he had succumbed to corruption through ambition and greed. Maybe he was naive and morally weak. Maybe, after the struggle to reach where he was, he felt justified in reaping his reward and gaining some economic security. Gradually he conformed to the way a mukhia was expected to behave, both by the officials and other mukhias he now worked with on the one hand, and the villagers on the other. He could not stand alone.

Since then I have seen a similar pattern repeated where a poor, well-meaning, more educated villager ends up joining the forces of exploitation. That is why it is so important to focus on programmes that benefit the community as a whole and not certain individuals within it.

21

The Politics of Hunger

The main problem for the villagers is food. They grow only one crop of paddy a year and, as there are no irrigation facilities, the success of the crop depends on the monsoon. Even in a good year there are few families who are able to feed themselves for the whole year. On 16 August 1981, I wrote home, 'The rain is not plentiful this year and so transplanting is late. It's a bad lookout if the fields don't fill up with water soon. The villagers still seem quite hopeful.' But, unfortunately, that hope was misplaced; the 1981 harvest was a disaster. Many families had consumed all their paddy within a week or two. And then it was a question of surviving each day with whatever they could manage to earn or with any fruit and grasses that could be found. Opportunities for earning were very scarce and soon many of the menfolk were leaving the villages in search of work further afield. Many families subsisted solely on the meagre proceeds of selling the leaf plates made by the women and children. The moneylenders increased their stranglehold and deforestation accelerated at an alarming rate—trees were cut down and sold, or stolen. Even while living among them, it was difficult to understand how the villagers survived.

As the food crisis was so acute and widespread, it seemed to us that it was the government's responsibility to do something to alleviate the situation. The area had been officially declared a drought-affected area. We paid a visit to the BDO. He was a self-confident young man and was outwardly very friendly towards us. On hearing of our concern, he leaned back in his chair laughing and assured us that no one here would starve. Manan pointed out that doctors don't write 'starvation' as a cause of death on a death certificate. Our idea at this stage was to apply for cheap flour to make into chapattis to sell with vegetables—to set up a cheap food-stall. In theory, cheap grain was available from the government dealers but it was sold on the black market. Apparently we could be supplied with wheat rations if we sold it in a cooked form.

Nearly two months passed after we had submitted our application. We had paid several more visits to the BDO, but no action whatsoever had been taken. During this time we had also been having meetings and discussions with the villagers and, at the beginning of February, we started in earnest. We wanted to explain to the villagers that we could not—nor would it be right for us—provide a solution to the problem. It was up to them to approach the government themselves. We talked to them about the working of the government and about the taxes they pay. Together we decided to hold a three-day sit-in demonstration outside the block offices from 16 to 18 February to demand foodgrain at the government-controlled rate and work opportunities in the villages.

Over a period of two weeks, I arranged and attended more than twenty women's meetings in different villages. The response was impressive. At first I called together the women in Titmoh and most of them came in spite of the overcast weather. After I had spoken, they all started talking amongst themselves. They decided that one rupee should be collected from each household and made Debimaya responsible for collection. They quickly became very active, accompanying me to other villages, often a good distance away, to talk to more women. Sometimes we were out all day long, some women carrying their babies with them. At one meeting almost the entire female population of Sonajori village came and handed over the money they had collected in front of the Fatepur women, prompting them to offer their contributions too. The women are used to going to the forest together to collect leaves and firewood, and also to the market. Perhaps this helps explain why they took more spontaneously to collective action than the men. Some of the men, though, including the health workers, were very active too. Somra, for example, had, within a few days, grown confident enough to talk to the villagers at length in Santhali, putting the message across in his own way. We were not allied to any political party, only '*pet ka party* (the tummy's party),' he would say.

Our final meeting in Titmoh before the demonstration was attended by more than five hundred villagers. By then the villagers had managed to collect about Rs 500 to help pay for their food during the three days. Some rumours were circulating that we would be fired on by the police in Madhupur, be forcibly sterilized and that I was collecting villagers to fight wars in my country!

From early morning on 16 February, we could hear the distant beating of drums—the Santhals were calling the people together. The sound gradually grew louder. Villagers assembled in four villages and marched along different routes, converging on a place about one mile from the block offices. From there they set off in two orderly lines, with drums beating at the head of the procession and at intervals down the line, carrying placards and shouting slogans.

'There is drought, we are hungry! Give us work, give us rations!'

'Santhals, Ghutvals, Muslims are one, everyone's hunger is the same!'

There were about a thousand villagers from fifty villages and more than half were women. There were villagers from all the different groups and communities; there were the very old and the very young, and there were cripples. Their demands were for food-for-work schemes, rice and wheat at controlled rates, and cheap flour for chapatti shops.

The BDO came out of his office in the evening to talk to them. He tried to explain that he was doing all he could and was dependent on his superiors, but the villagers were not impressed and were not about to be humoured so easily. When a twelve-year-old boy began to talk, the BDO cut him short saying that he was talking about work with the adults and the boy should be at school. At this the boy retorted that he was capable of more work than the BDO and someone else pointed out that he could not go to school when he had no food.

On the morning of the seventeenth and eighteenth the villagers held meetings among themselves and the general feeling was that the BDO had tried to bluff them. At the last meeting Bagloo (one of the health workers) spoke movingly. He asked everyone what they had gained from these three days. He said that they had gained unity which was far more valuable than anything money could buy. He said that we had to tell everyone when we went home that we had not been fired upon by the police and had not been sterilized. By the time the sit-in ended, everyone was very tired and several of the women had fallen ill. But there was not a murmur of complaint. We really felt that a new spirit of unity and determination had grown amongst them. Those who had said at the beginning that we would need two months to prepare for the demonstration, that the villagers should not be away from home for three days and that it would not be possible for them to make contributions, had misjudged the spirit of the people. Even among the tired, the weak and the old, that spirit had remained strong. Both Manan and I felt that we had grown much closer to the villagers. We had made many new contacts, and with our old friends like Debimaya, our relationship was now based less on dependence and more on equality, greater understanding and respect.

Madhupur had never seen a demonstration like this before, one which the villagers felt was theirs. There was some press coverage. In a letter that was published in the *Weekly Guardian* (London) I drew attention to the fact that while the villagers were staging their demonstration, the Indian government was concluding a $1.3 billion deal with France to buy forty advanced Mirage-2000 fighter-bombers. 'When the government exports foodstuffs to help pay for arms and does not take action to prevent its citizens dying of starvation, just what are the Mirage bombers intended to defend? Not the standard of living apparently, nor a standard of morality,' I wrote.

No significant action was taken and so our campaign in the villages continued. We planned to help organize the whole block of five hundred villages but for this we needed more people with energy and commitment. As the food situation was deteriorating day by day, it became still more difficult for the villagers to do anything other than struggle to get a daily meal. Even so some villagers continued tirelessly to go long distances on foot and by bicycle, in the now scorching sun and hot wind, to spread the news about what was happening. We scaled down our plans and arranged a three-day march around the southern part of the block. As before, it was the women who were most active. Villagers whom we had never met before welcomed us and put us up for the night and, on one occasion, made a collection to buy tea. One elderly Dalit woman, Nunia Devi, who had previously been silently supportive, found her voice, began to take part in meetings and got up to explain events to the others in fluent detail.

Since, in spite of all our efforts and in spite of going to see the district commissioner in Dumka and the governor of Bihar in Patna, no adequate measures were being taken by the government to prevent a famine, we decided to go to Patna with a group of villagers. Manan and I selected the villagers, explaining to them that we felt this was the best and simplest way. It was also agreed that they would pay half the expenses through a village collection and we would pay the other half. We aimed at having an equal number of men and women of different castes, representing different villages from Madhupur block and that they should be people who are able to express themselves. There were five men and five women, two of them with babies. The women included one Muslim, one Dalit, one Ghutval and two Mohlines. The males included two Santhals, two Ghutval and one Pujar. We tried to impress upon them that they should not be intimidated by unfamiliar surroundings and explained about things like latrines and traffic.

Out of the train window on the way to Patna, they were surprised to see so many crops growing in the fields. Huge mounds of wheat were being harvested. We explained that the land and wheat did not belong to the villagers but only to a few rich landowners and that many of the villagers here had no land and worked as labourers for very low wages.

On arriving in Patna, we set off together to walk the couple of miles to the house of our friend, Mr Kumar. Everything was new to them. It was also odd and new for the people of Patna to see us and a little crowd gathered around, listening attentively to our answers to their questions.

We arrived at Mr Kumar's house at about 3 p.m. and were greeted by his wife as he was out. She gave everyone tea on the veranda. Mr Kumar had left us the contact numbers of some useful people. We tried to get in touch with them but were not successful. Using the phone in Patna was seldom a rewarding experience. We decided to try our luck with meeting the Governor of Bihar whom I had met once earlier, though not without great difficulty in making an appointment. The first obstacle was the police at the gate. To my surprise on this occasion, after the requisite phone call from the gate to the mansion and a short wait, I was accompanied down the long driveway through the well-tended gardens. Once there, one of the turbaned, tunic-clad bearers showed me where to wait. I had not expected that I would be allowed to meet the Governor immediately and was not feeling at all presentable in these grand surroundings after our long, hot journey.

When I was shown in he immediately asked me if there had been any results in the village since our last meeting. I explained that nothing significant had happened and that I had met the district commissioner as he had suggested, but did not feel that he had taken the matter to heart. I mentioned that we had now come with some villagers. He said it would not be appropriate for him to see them as it would look as if he was bypassing the government. When I asked for his advice as to whom it would be best for the villagers to meet and how to go about it, he suggested the chief minister and the relief minister, Mr L.P. Sahi.

As Mr Sahi's residence was nearby we decided to go there. This whole area of Patna is extremely grand, with wide leafy avenues, on either side of which are stately residences of the various government ministers set in ample grounds. Mr Sahi was out. We were told to try again in the morning at ten. By the time we returned to Mr Kumar's house, the villagers were eating the meal they had prepared by the side of the house. Then they settled down to sleep on the veranda.

It was interesting to hear the reactions of the Kumars and

their friends to our idea of bringing the villagers to Patna. Mrs Kumar told us in no uncertain terms that she thought we were wasting our time and money, and that no government ministers were interested in helping the poor. Mr Kumar's friend agreed. But Mr Kumar himself supported us, partly because he felt that we were the best people to judge what was right in the situation. We tried to explain that it was not with the idea of begging for help that we had come, but with the idea that if the government is not prepared to help, the villagers should see and understand this for themselves. For one thing, it would be an educational experience for them which they could make use of in shaping their future struggles, and for another, we could use the opportunity to increase publicity about the situation and the government's lack of response. A very positive and important result of all this, which became more and more apparent, was the way our efforts together helped to strengthen the motivation and fellow-feeling of the villagers.

Not that everything between them always went smoothly. In fact the next morning there were ructions because some had disappeared and those that remained said they had gone to see the Ganga down the road. It turned out there had been a misunderstanding and that this was not so—they had gone in search of a place to go to the toilet as there was a long queue outside the latrine.

We were all present at the chief minister's *janta darbar* (peoples' court) before 9 a.m. It was a covered area with rows of benches beside his residence where he met the people in the morning. There were a variety of people waiting, mostly quite well-dressed, each with a piece of paper in hand.

The chief minister was late and did not make his appearance till after 10.30 a.m. Then he moved swiftly down the rows, exchanging hardly a few words with each supplicant and collecting the papers which he mechanically handed to his assistant. The first member of our group he reached was the elderly Dalit woman. The conversation ran approximately as follows:

Chief minister: Where is she from?
Old woman: From Madhupur, Dumka district.
C.M.: Why from so far?
Old woman: There is famine, sir, our paddy has died.
C.M.: Famine? Go away. Go away.

When it became obvious that none of the villagers was going to get a hearing, Manan moved forward and spoke in English. At this the chief minister hesitated and paid more attention. He took a copy of our memorandum and the newspaper cuttings and said that instructions would be given on the matter that very day.

After this fiasco I had arranged to meet the members of the Bihar assembly, which was in session at the time. It was too late to go to Mr Sahi, the relief minister by then. When Manan arrived with the villagers at the assembly, however, they were not allowed through the outer gate. But when I arrived I sailed right up to the entrance of the assembly building and was puzzled not to find them there. I, a foreigner, had no difficulty but the people of the country were stopped at the gate! When we eventually managed to meet up, I led them in. A nice policeman allowed Manan and me inside the building while the villagers waited by the steps. We went to see Mr Karpoori Thakur, ex-chief minister and leader of the opposition. He was welcoming and responsive. He, like the Governor, had never received the latest memorandum we had sent by registered post ten days before. If he had, he said, he would have included the matter in his main speech to the assembly. He explained that he would not be able to meet the villagers that day but invited them to his residence at 8 a.m. the next day.

When we came out, the villagers were not where we had left them. The police had chased them away! Debimaya was cross with the others for not standing their ground.

Then we set off with them to various newspaper offices. At the Press Trust of India (PTI) office Manan and I first went in to explain who we were, asking the villagers to wait at the entrance. We hadn't yet managed to convince the rather supercilious young man we found there that I was not a missionary and that it was not relevant to the matter in hand which country I came from and how long I had been here, when the villagers appeared at the door. Someone else had invited them inside. But this was too much for the young man who lost no time in telling them to leave. So we also left. After that experience our reception at the *Indian Express* office came as a pleasant surprise. The man there, Mr Kripakaran, although busy reporting the proceedings at the assembly, spent nearly an hour with us and interviewed three of the villagers with patience and genuine concern mingled with wry humour directed at the government. He suggested that we try to meet a Mr Saxsena. Mr Saxsena was an unusual government official, a man of principles and integrity. He had previously been district commissioner of Dhanbad, a mining city notorious for its gangsters and corruption. He was moved from there after attempts on his life. We arrived at his residence about 6 p.m. We waited till after 8 p.m. but he did not appear, so we reluctantly gave up. Some curious boys asked us why we were sitting there and when they heard whom we were waiting to see they confirmed that he was a special sort of government officer. Although he had the use of a car, they said, he always walked to and from work.

As it was getting late, Somra and I went back by rickshaw to light the fire for supper while the others followed on foot. When we arrived, we found that one of Mr Kumar's friends was waiting to take Manan and me to a hotel to meet a

Mr Madhu Mehta. As soon as Manan arrived we were whisked away on the back of his scooter. We found ourselves tired and dirty-footed, entering a very posh hotel. We had already heard of Mr Mehta, who is convenor of *Hindustani Andolan* and it so happened he was passing through Patna that night. We were introduced. He was a rather odd-looking large man, with longish hair but bald on top and rather deaf. We talked about our work and why we had come to Patna. He knew Mr Kripakaran, the man at the *Indian Express,* and immediately called him, asking him to be sure to publish something. He instructed his two assistants who were present to visit us in the village in order to report to him about the situation on the spot.

In the morning the villagers got up very early and went to have a bath in the Ganga; all but Somra who stayed behind to wash the pans. (The leaf plates they ate off were disposable. We had been obliged to buy them at the rate of five rupees per hundred although when they made them, they sold them for only fifty paise to one rupee per hundred.) They set off on foot to Mr Karpoori Thakur's residence as the way was now familiar to them and we followed later. We sat on the lawn outside his grand residence. A little crowd of visitors had already assembled. A small boy was distributing tea and gave some to Manan and me, differentiating us, we thought, from the villagers. But we were wrong—there was a shortage of glasses and the boy later gave tea to everyone. When Karpoori Thakur arrived, he called us inside and had chairs arranged for all of us, women first. Manan and I sat at the back. I can still visualize the scene. Karpoori Thakur stood in front of the seated villagers surrounded by followers and supplicants, and at first directed his words to Manan. Before Manan had finished his reply, the old Dalit woman who was the first to have been brushed aside by the chief minister, started to speak. She explained in detail their hunger, how they cooked the little rice they had with a large amount of salty water in order to fill their stomachs, and their unsuccessful attempts to make the government do something for them. Everyone listened in silence as she talked confidently and fluently. A few of the others made some comments. Another woman mentioned that the villagers had made a collection to pay for their expenses for coming to Patna. Karpoori Thakur gave assurances that he would do whatever he could and would raise the matter in the assembly. Before we left, Manan thanked him for his reception and for giving the villagers tea and chairs. He also explained that we appreciated his concern, yet ultimately we did not depend on anyone at the top, we depended on the villagers themselves.

From Karpoori Thakur's it was not far down the spacious green avenue to the residence of Mr Lahtan Choudhary, minister of supplies. The villagers waited on the grass verge outside. Inside, the waiting room was full of dhoti-clad men with large bellies. We wrote our names on a paper that was taken in and a little later we were shown in. It was quite impossible to imagine the villagers entering the place. They belonged to a different world. Any attempt on their part to directly communicate with this world would surely have been met with embarrassment and consternation. The minister of supplies was an unsmiling gentleman. His mind must have continued to run along the same lines after we left him as it had been before we met. That is to say, he gave no indication that the news of hungry villagers who receive no rations had in any way disturbed the pattern of his thoughts. He would issue instructions. There was a shortage of rice but it might be possible to supply wheat.

After this we went to Mr L.P. Sahi with the feeling that it would simply not be possible for the villagers to talk to a minister face to face. Karpoori Thakur's behaviour had been different. As an opposition leader it was in his interest to hear complaints about the government but, apart from this, he was, by all accounts, a veteran politician of a different calibre. We went to Mr L.P. Sahi's secretary who told us that they had been expecting us at 10 a.m. the day before. We explained that we had been delayed at the chief minister's and had not realized that a definite appointment had been made for us. The secretary seemed a pleasant man. He said he would inform the minister so that we could meet him when he came home for lunch and that it would certainly be possible for the villagers to meet him also.

While the villagers waited outside his residence, Manan and I decided to go in search of Mr Saxsena who would be in his office at this time. We went first to the New Secretariat building but were stopped immediately at the gate by a policeman. I went to another gate alone and the policeman there was more inclined to make an exception for a foreigner. I went back to call Manan but the policeman wasn't happy about that. At this point an elderly little man intervened and said he would escort us to the labour commissioner (we understood that Mr Saxsena was the labour commissioner). When we found the office closed, he invited us to sit and wait in the comfort of his own office across the way and ordered tea. He did all this in a very friendly, matter-of-fact way and didn't ply us with any questions but set busily about the files on his desk. We ventured to interrupt to confirm that the labour commissioner was indeed Mr Saxsena. This turned out not to be the case, but, he said, we would first have tea and sort it out after that, and he continued to sign his papers. When the tea arrived, he sat back and relaxed and tentatively asked why we had come. He also spoke highly of Mr Saxsena and told us his office was in the Old Secretariat. Before we left we exchanged addresses—he was under-secretary to the minister of agriculture and he said he would visit us some time.

We had to wait a while at the Old Secretariat before we were taken up the grand, wide staircase to his office. As the door was opened to let us in I caught sight of a second figure in the room. I didn't immediately recognize him but at the mere sight of him an unpleasant feeling came over me. I realized who he was just in time to whisper to Manan that it was the district commissioner from Dumka whom I had been to see about the famine about a week earlier. He was probably one of the reasons why nothing was happening for the villagers. It was an extremely awkward situation. We had come to introduce ourselves to and seek the assistance of Mr Saxsena as a representative of the all-too-few honest and sincere government officials, while sitting there beside him was a representative of corruption and indifference! Mr Saxsena looked different from the mental picture I had developed of him. He was quite young, and his face expressed concentration and tension rather than the serene austerity I had expected. It was very difficult to talk in front of the district commissioner. I said we had been referred by Mr Kripakaran. He showed no sign of knowing him. I began to explain about the impending famine. He indicated the district commissioner sitting beside him. I said I recognized him. He said this was not his domain and we should meet the relief commissioner, and he said it in such a way as to show that he did not want to continue the matter.

At midday we were waiting with the villagers under a tree in front of Mr Sahi's residence. You could tell when he was arriving by the sudden flurry of activity among the people clustered around the front door. He paused to talk to them, then looked across at us. He came towards us and we talked standing under the tree. In appearance he was no different from the other fat ministers. Mr Sahi mentioned that the Governor had phoned him and told him about us the same day that I had seen him. He seemed to grasp what the situation required quickly and began to dictate a note of instructions in Hindi about supply of rations and food-for-work schemes. When he asked the names of the villages members of our group had come from, we explained that they had come on behalf of the villagers of the whole block and he stopped noting down the names. He assured us that measures would be taken in the first week of April. We felt more satisfied after the meeting although Manan and I discouraged the villagers from being too hopeful.

After this the villagers made their way to the station. We met them there after having said our goodbyes and our thanks to Mr Kumar and his family, and popped in to see Mr Kripakaran again to let him know the outcome of our meeting with Mr Sahi. Our idea was that Mr Sahi's assurances should also be published in his article for the *Indian Express*. We set off home with the feeling that our voice had been heard. It remained to be seen if it would result in anything concrete.

On our return I wrote to Mr Saxsena to explain who we were and why we had gone to see him. We made another unsuccessful attempt to meet him in Patna in May. Towards the end of May he was transferred from his influential position to a lesser one. I also wrote to the Governor thanking him for his help and sent a copy of the letter to Mr L.P. Sahi so that he would know that the Governor had been informed of his assurances.

Two articles appeared in the newspapers. There was a forceful one by Mr Kripakaran in the *Indian Express* entitled 'Bihar government deaf to the cries of the semi-starved' and the other was in a Hindi daily *Aryavarta*. Mr G.S. Sinha, a friend of Mr Madhu Mehta, came to Titmoh and wrote a report following which Mr Mehta wrote a letter to Prime Minister Indira Gandhi about the villagers' situation.

Nothing happened in the first week of April nor even by

the beginning of May. At the end of May some rations were distributed—1 kg rice per family and 5 kg of rotten, bitter-tasting flour at rates only slightly less than the market price. It was no more than a show. But at least the authorities had felt obliged to make a show! Some wells and dams were also constructed but this did not provide employment on anything like the scale required. Sometimes stone-dust was substituted for cement and dams were built in places with a very small catchment area, by the roadside, so that they could be easily seen by a passing official. The BDO made good money. It was said that he regularly subtracted for himself 30 per cent of the amount sanctioned.

Towards the end of May Manan and I made another trip to Patna. We met the Governor again and also the relief commissioner (as Mr Saxsena had suggested), a pleasant man who spoke frankly about the extent of corruption. We met Mr L.P. Sahi again but he did not impress us. His previous performance appeared to have been merely for show.

We also met the famous Mr Saxsena again. This time we were able to talk freely. He gave us tea but he drank only hot water himself. He apologized profusely for what had happened at the secretariat and explained that, in the circumstances, he couldn't arrange a meeting elsewhere. Even amid the general callousness, complacency and corruption, it was possible to find someone with higher ideals. How much of his striving was for change in society and how much for adherence to principle in his own life, I do not know. No doubt the two were intertwined.

In a village meeting on 16 May (three months after our big demonstration in Madhupur), we reviewed the events. Faced with the government's apathy, the villagers expressed the need to organize themselves. The 'chair' of the Bihar government was symbolically burnt.

I have related here the events that took place during the

first half of 1982. Although we were unsuccessful in our immediate aims, our efforts had some interesting consequences. As far as the villagers themselves were concerned, the sense of unity and common purpose which grew during the course of the campaign made us all aware of qualities that had, till then, remained dormant. It was not an easy or a quick process. We wanted to avoid their dependence on us as decision-makers. We saw ourselves as allies and friends, not leaders. Of course there were those villagers who had tagged along more out of opportunism than a real understanding of the situation: 'You had us running around a lot and what did we get?' they would say to us. On the other hand, there were some individuals who had gained confidence in their collective strength. It was here, rather than in the size of meetings and processions, that the success of our efforts lay.

The authorities reacted predictably by singling us out as troublemakers. Posters appeared in Madhupur accusing us of being CIA agents and an article was published in a local newspaper entitled 'Foreign girl misguiding labour force'. I was supposedly obstructing government relief programmes that were 'in full swing'! We were not sure how to react. A little later I learnt that the politician quoted in the article was visiting Madhupur. I decided to confront him in person. I set off to see him in the dak bungalow more with a sense of amusement and bravado than in anger. I went alone, unannounced and found him surrounded in the usual way by his followers. I proceeded to introduce myself and challenged him in Hindi to substantiate the allegations against me. He found himself in an awkward position as he knew nothing about me apart from the falsehoods that had been fed to him, no doubt by the BDO. He hedged and consulted his supporters. After a while he rallied and asked me if there were any poor people in my country and why didn't I help them! The interview came to an abrupt end when he suddenly got up and led his followers away, leaving me sitting where I was. I took it as a sign of capitulation and felt satisfied that he had been suitably humbled.

We began to take precautions for our safety and, in particular, were careful when cycling on the road to get well clear as soon as we heard a vehicle approaching. When the villagers became aware of the threats against us their response was immediate and touching. A group of them came to us one day armed with bows and arrows and axes. Within the villages they would defend us with their lives, they said, but in the world beyond we had to take care of ourselves.

*

The allegations against us were predictable and, to some extent, an indication of our success, but other consequences were less predictable and served to undermine the unity we were striving to build.

When I had first arrived in the village, I had known of no other groups working in the area. This was no longer the case. I had been pleased to become acquainted with a group of young men in Madhupur who were active in the movement launched by Jayprakash Narayan. A couple of years before the events described here, I had introduced them to a well-known aid organization naively expecting that some financial support would help them translate their ideas into practical benefits for the villagers. Being aware of the advantages of working together, we had, from the outset of our campaign, gone out of our way to include this group in our discussions and decision-making. They did not attend the village meetings but joined us at the demonstration in Madhupur, where they were very active in helping with arrangements to prepare food for such a large number of people.

The success of the demonstration we had organized with

the villagers no doubt took them by surprise. It prompted them to engage in earnest in what the villagers very aptly called '*leaderi*'. They now became busy organizing meetings themselves, without any reference to us, in which they urged the villagers, we were told, to 'follow' them as they were local people, not foreigners! Thinking that we were working together, the villagers became confused and some were very angry. By now the group was receiving substantial amounts of funding from the aid organization, had established an office in Madhupur and purchased a motorbike. They organized some workshops and seminars on topics such as 'social forestry' although it was not entirely clear how these benefited the poor villagers who were struggling to get food each day. No doubt it was an idea thought up by some 'development consultant' in a smart office in the city.

The term 'development consultant' makes me distinctly queasy. Maybe my experiences have made me too cynical about aid organizations but it seems to me that this term has been thought up by some middle-class individuals who may have good intentions but have little understanding of poverty. The fashionable concept of 'empowerment' seems the ideal excuse to make an interesting career out of organizing talk shops and expounding on how to improve villagers' lives without actually doing anything.

It happened that one such 'development consultant' was related to the field director of the organization which was supporting the Madhupur group. The following year she published an article entitled 'Rules of Real Aid No. 2: Mobilize the Poor' in the *New Internationalist,* a well-known magazine in the UK dealing with Third World issues. The article extolled the work of this group and included a description of our demonstration, which they were credited with having organized! It is a nice story, written with imagination, but unfortunately does not bear much relation to actual events. The deception of the article was further compounded by the photograph that appeared with it, which purported to be of the villagers' demonstration. It was a little while before we discovered its source. We later found a pamphlet on the Bombay textile workers strike at the Calcutta Book Fair with the very same photograph on its cover. Not having a genuine photograph of the villagers' demonstration, she, or the magazine's editor, had used one of the Bombay textile workers instead!

The dishonesty and deception of this article were shocking and the idea of mobilizing the poor like so many sheep was not one we would have sought to promote or convey. We did not challenge its authenticity at the time as we did not want to put ourselves or our work at risk. I did, however, make some discreet enquiries about the level of financial support the group was receiving and was amazed by what I learnt. Obviously mobilizing the poor is an expensive business!

Binay Singh, my friend in Madhupur, used to say that aid organizations take money from the poor of the rich countries and give it to the rich of the poor countries! He was engaging in hyperbole but it is an unfortunate fact that the receipt of large amounts of funds can have a very corrupting and detrimental effect. Fund-raising tends to become an end in itself and glowing reports, whether faithfully reflecting reality or not, are often seen as necessary by project workers and donor organizations alike. Such misleading reports obscure the reality about what is happening. The desire for funds tempts one to seek quick or short-term results—more easily achieved by working with better-off villagers, increasing existing inequalities in the process. Funding and the accompanying paraphernalia like offices and jeeps only serves to create greater distance from the poor. As dependence on funding grows and larger amounts are at stake, the recipients are less likely to be prepared to 'rock the boat' and seek to bring about changes in the status quo which might lead to real benefits for the poor.

The activities of groups seeking to carve out their piece of empire in the development business was yet another obstacle which we encountered in the course of our work. We look forward to the day when villagers draw their strength and solidarity from each other, and not from any outsider. When they can write their own story. But I'm afraid it will be a long time coming.

22

The Search for Solutions

Faced with the villagers' poverty and hunger, it is easy to become beguiled by the idea that, if only we could find it, there must be a solution to the problem: a higher-yielding rice crop, a simple and cheap form of irrigation, a new type of fertilizer or an 'income-generating' scheme that will take off and bring in the much-needed cash. Like the alchemists of the Middle Ages who sought to change base metals into gold, we too search for a magic formula. The search is that much more tantalizing because we seem to know the fragments of a solution, but as we try to put them together, they begin to fall apart.

Kitchen Gardens

When I first moved to the village, I found that the volunteers who had been working there before me had provided for a walled kitchen garden with irrigation facilities. On the face of it, this seemed a very good idea, especially as the problems of both protection and irrigation had been solved. A large area, protected from goats and other animals by a brick wall, had been divided into plots for different families to cultivate. There was an irrigation well twenty feet in diameter beside each kitchen garden and the water was raised by means of a Persian wheel (buckets attached to a revolving chain) operated by bullocks. Expertise on the growing of vegetables was on hand from the project agriculturalist. And yet the project was a failure. True, a few villagers did grow some vegetables, but, in general, the land was not utilized to anything like the extent one might have expected.

It would be easy to say that the reason for this failure was the villagers' apathy and laziness, but there were other reasons. The villagers do not consider growing vegetables a priority. For them it was a bit like providing butter when you have no bread. The poorest did not have bullocks to turn the Persian wheel to raise water from the well. Although the technology provided was 'appropriate' in the sense that it did not require materials or technicians from outside the village, it still did not meet the needs of the poorest villagers.

After only a few years, the walled garden had fallen into disuse. Manan and I decided to try and resurrect the project by making it a collective venture. The idea that the land should be cultivated jointly, initially between eight families, was greeted with enthusiasm. Immediately the problem of the lack of bullocks was resolved as it was decided that the eight would turn the wheel themselves, four on each side of the bar. It was decided to grow a staple crop, potatoes. We would provide the seed and they would repay us at harvest time. One villager in the group, Debimaya's husband Jailal, who never used to speak in meetings, became quite vocal. The group even started talking about cultivating some of the land outside the garden!

Inevitably, the initial enthusiasm began to wane and some friction developed between the participants. Some were enthusiastic and hard-working, but others did not turn up for work when they were meant to. We worked hard to foster a collective spirit and help to ensure they made decisions together. When one villager, Titua, wanted to leave because others were not pulling their weight, Manan talked to him for a long time to encourage him to help the group work together rather than opt out of it.

In spite of our efforts and limited success, the collective gardening project did not take off. Now, years later, the kitchen gardens are a sad sight. The walls have fallen down and the Persian wheels are rusted and broken. The provision of facilities to help the villagers improve their diet had, in the end, come to nothing.

The Leaf Plate Machine

Leaf plate making was a traditional occupation of the women. The leaf plates were sold to middlemen in town, and used in restaurants and festivals. Some enterprising individual in the city developed a leaf-plate machine which, using the plates the women made by hand, produced a plate of superior quality and higher market value. The machine consisted of a metal frame standing about five feet high with a mould attached at the top. A foot-operated pedal at the bottom acted to raise and lower the upper part of the mould. Two leaf plates with a piece of plastic between them were introduced by the operator and a kerosene burner heated the mould so that the plastic melted, fixing the two plates together. A sharp downward movement on the pedal cut the now strengthened and waterproof plate into shape. Several moulds were available for fashioning large, medium and small plates, and large and small bowls.

We invested in two of these machines, and for a time one of our rooms was a hive of activity as one person operated the machine and another cut the plastic into the required size. The third person supplied the leaf plates and the plastic to the operator and trimmed and packed the newly made plates. One of the villagers we employed was Dhano, a quiet young man who was unable to do any strenuous work as his heart had been severely damaged by rheumatic fever. He was delighted at being able to earn and help his hard-pressed wife. The women we bought the leaf plates from were pleased to receive a higher rate and to skip the travel to town to sell them.

The production side was well organized. Market outlets were there, but in the larger towns a long way away. The problem for us proved to be transporting the plates and securing a regular buyer. We did sell a good number, mainly in Calcutta, but the rate of sale did not keep pace with the rate of production. We did not make a loss in spite of being overwhelmed with unsold plates. Ideally we needed someone to take charge of the marketing of the plates but it was not possible to find such a person in the village. Promotion and marketing on this scale was not feasible for them. It fell to us and we were too preoccupied with other activities. Once again a seemingly good and 'appropriate' programme foundered, not for lack of technology but from lack of appropriate manpower.

The Wind Pump

For years I had dreamt of building an irrigation pump powered by wind. Lack of irrigation facilities was a major obstacle to saving the rice crop from the vagaries of the weather and to extending the growing season beyond the monsoon. The only form of pump used by the better-off villagers was a diesel pump. Otherwise they relied on lifting water manually. This was either a one-man operation using a weighted pole to dip a bucket into a hole in the ground, or two people rhythmically slung water from one level to another using a tarred basket with rope attached to each side.

At certain times of the year, the wind was very strong and the possibility of putting it to good use worked on me for a long time. My researches led me up many blind alleys. Some machines were too expensive while others not robust and effective enough to be worthwhile. I eventually managed to track down the author of a pamphlet on the 'Savonius Rotor' published several years earlier by the Centre for Alternative Technology in Wales. Although he had never travelled further than France before, John kindly agreed to spend a few weeks in the village in 1988 to investigate prospects for small-scale water pumping to irrigate a second crop after the paddy harvest. Managing to overcome his culture shock, his lack of any knowledge of Hindi and doubts arising from his natural humility, John first spent his time in the village watching and observing. After considering the various options (water, steam and wind power) and monitoring the wind speed (only 8–10 mph at that time of the year) and direction (fairly constant), he decided to construct a portable Cretan-style wind pump. The basic frame—in a pyramid shape with one side vertical—was made from lengths of bamboo lashed together. It was only ten feet tall—as, for the pump to be portable, the rotor had to be within reach for easy removal. The rotor was ten feet in diameter and had eight arms which bore eight canvas sails. The sails would turn a shaft, the further end of which would carry a crank to work the piston of the pump. Two circular hardwood chapatti boards were clamped together to make the brake. A few necessary items were brought from Calcutta.

Villagers crowded around, some for part of the day, others for all of it, to watch and participate as the machine gradually took shape. It took just over two weeks to build. When transported to an open area by the stream it took a quarter of an hour to set up and the sails turned with only a slight wind. At a wind speed of 8 to 10 mph, it delivered 190-210 gallons of water per hour, raising water from six to seven feet. The cost of the pump, at that time, came to Rs 1420.

Here was a simple, relatively cheap machine which pumped

water by itself with no running costs at all. But the villagers did not react with joy. The machine was completely new. It was neither the familiar noisy, efficient diesel pump disgorging many gallons of water each hour nor was it the simple hand-operated tarred basket. It was hard for them to assimilate it into their way of doing things.

And there were no doubt other factors, like the fact that the season with the greatest wind did not correspond to the growing season. In order to make the most of the relatively little wind at that time of the year, the machine probably needed to be taller but therefore more cumbersome and less portable. Or, at any rate, it had to be in a wide open space to catch what wind there was. Thora, one villager who was particularly interested, tried to use the wind pump on his more sheltered piece of land and, sadly, it did not work.

Before coming John had written, 'With most alternative technology machines, we have to lower our sights a little or a long way from the high expectations conditioned by our very high technology. In other words we cannot overload our home-made machines and expect them to work. We must trim our needs to our means.' Were the villagers' expectations too high in spite of their poverty?

Even so, I feel we did not have the chance to give it a fair trial. Given more time and perseverance it could have achieved a degree of acceptance and use. After all, it took years for the oral-rehydration packets and IUDs to become a part of their lives.

The building of the machine led John to reflect upon the experience of the villagers witnessing the step-by-step construction of a new machine and the interest that this had generated. This, as much as the finished product itself, could, he thought, be a catalyst for change. He was moved to donate the tools he had used most of his adult life to the villagers. He wrote, 'If it is tools that have made possible material change in the world—from the Bronze Age to the Industrial Revolution—then perhaps it will be tools that will induce a lurch in attitude towards change here.'

An Efficient Stove

In response to the fuel crisis we set about building a more fuel-efficient stove from a design we found in a book. Several designs are available, all of them an improvement on the traditional primitive stove the villagers use where a great deal of heat is wasted and there is no chimney for the smoke to escape. Our stove was made out of slabs made from mud reinforced with chopped paddy straw which dried very hard in the sun. The only component needed from outside the village was the metal damper which controlled the amount of air entering the stove and hence the rate of burning. At first we made the chimney out of earthenware cylinders made by the local potter. The construction of the stove was labour intensive and not expensive. The holes for the cooking pots were made to fit individual pots so that no heat escaped around them. Another advantage over the traditional stove was that two pots could be heated at the same time.

The stove generated a good amount of interest. Having made a few myself, I managed after some time to train Debimaya and she, along with another villager, Chandolal, continued the work. We charged a small fee for each stove. Gradually the demand for them increased until one day disaster struck. A villager's thatched roof caught fire from the chimney. On this occasion we made the chimney out of tin as it was cheaper and we had avoided the delay of waiting for the potter. Although the villagers readily agreed that the modification would prevent such accidents in future, the general unresponsiveness to change made it hard to put this incident behind us. However, as so often happened, one or two individuals remained firm in their support of the new idea. One responsive and intelligent Santhali woman living not far from our centre was very pleased with her stove, and years after I had made it for her, she proudly showed me that it was still very much in use. She explained that it required half the amount of firewood as compared to her previous stove which meant that instead of going to collect firewood every four days, she now had to go only once every eight days.

Perhaps with greater perseverance and promotion these new ideas might have taken hold. Perhaps we withdrew too soon. Our ability to put sustained efforts into these ventures was inevitably limited by our preoccupation with our health work. More importantly, we did not feel it was our role to cajole the villagers into accepting them. We introduced some new possibilities and it was up to them to adopt them. In the end there were few tangible results but perhaps some seeds of change were sown. Our efforts can be seen not so much as failures but as part of a process from which we all could learn.

23

Two Worlds Meet

Over the last few years, here and there, pukka buildings have been built in the villages by the government to serve as community rooms, schools or even health posts. They remain neglected, empty shells, sometimes half-built (presumably the contractor went off with the rest of the money) and stick out like sore thumbs amongst the mud houses which blend harmoniously with the countryside. The villagers, with a smile, call them 'nach ghar' or dance houses, using the roof to spread chillies, mahua flowers and millet out to dry, away from the ubiquitous goats. It is tempting to see these buildings as symbols of 'development', well-intentioned but inappropriate and ineffective gestures, or worse—as ugly, harmful excrecences from the outside world.

Poverty is not simply the absence of material possessions, a shortage of food and money, and lack of adequate housing. It is more than this—it is a way of life and a perception of the world. One of its key characteristics is the feeling that you have little or no control over your life. And this feeling is constantly being reinforced. When the rains fail and the paddy dies, when a storm comes and takes the roof off your house, when your baby dies of diarrhoea in a matter of hours, what can you do? Along with this feeling of helplessness comes a resigned acceptance, '*Bhagwan ke hath me* (Its in the hands of God),' is a common refrain. The villagers do not often get angry; they are more likely to shrug, pick up the pieces and carry on. There is no choice. They are quite aware of the benefits of brick houses, motorbikes and diesel pumps but see these things as part of another world, the world of the rich.

No doubt this attitude has a positive side to it and helps make their insecure lives more tolerable. It brings a certain sense of serenity and even contentment. It means they are not overburdened by regrets about the past, and worries and plans for the future; they live very much in the present. On the other hand, there is a negative side as their acceptance of disaster and injustice can lead to apathy, passivity and a lack of motivation to improve their lives. In a paradoxical way, the attitude that helps to keep them content also helps to keep them in poverty.

It seems to me that their serenity and dignity in the face of adversity also springs from their strong sense of reality and their closeness to the natural world. They live out their lives in tune with the changing seasons of the year, which determine the cycle of planting, growing and harvesting; building and repairing of houses; arranging weddings and festivals; the food they can eat and even the prevalence of disease. They calculate the passage of time from the phases of the moon, and the rising and the setting of the sun orders and limits their day's activities. They philosophically endure the heat of summer and the cold of winter, the pain of illness and childbirth, and the inevitability and ever present proximity of death.

They use whatever is available to them to the utmost. From the soil they make their houses, pots and tiles and grow their food, from the trees they make their beds, ploughs and doors, they make baskets and winnowers from bamboo, brushes from grasses and rope from homegrown jute. There is very little apart from salt, cloth, oil and iron (for plough ends and axe heads) for which they depend on the outside world. And here lies another paradox—despite their poverty, they are more self-sufficient in their day-to-day existence than those living in more developed societies who have delegated many aspects of their sophisticated lives to 'experts'.

Until recently the villagers' lives were largely isolated from the outside world. But now the outside world is intruding more and more. They find themselves increasingly constrained to leave the village in search of solutions that were previously found within their own community. The need for money makes more men leave in search of employment. Some go to the coal mines in West Bengal. This means separation from their families for a large part of the year. It also means a high risk of contracting TB, leprosy and STD which they bring back to the village. They leave to sell—leaf plates, datwan, brushes, fruit, vegetables—and to buy. Consumer products like bicycles, watches and radios are now in demand. As pressures on the land grow and extended families become divided leading to tensions, they seek resolution of disputes in the courts, when previously this would have taken place at a local gathering of villagers. Some villagers have become embroiled in lengthy and expensive lawsuits. Cases drag on for years and mean innumerable visits to the court, each visit requiring expense on fares and bribing clerks. The lure of modern medicine has undermined their faith in traditional methods of healing, both the use of herbal medicine and witchcraft. In serious cases they will often 'hedge their bets' by going to a quack or a doctor or a chemist and seeking the services of a maybe 'jungli doctor' till now as well. The medical care they receive is often of a dubious quality and, again, greatly diminishes their meagre resources. The skills of reading and writing are mastered by very few individuals and only a handful of the few children who attend the local government primary school graduate to secondary school. For those who do through perseverance, enterprise or luck, what they learn has little relevance to their way of life. It serves to alienate them from their people and eventually they join the ranks of the better-off and become party to exploiting the majority who remain illiterate and poor.

The outside world is coming to the villages. Contractors come and employ the villagers on minimal wages to exploit the resources around them: for hewing the rocks into pieces to be taken, crushed and used for road-building, for felling trees, for gathering leaves. Politicians come at election time for their votes and missionaries come to lure them to their flock with rations and the chance for their children to go to school. International health teams arrive out of the blue one day to immunize children against a certain disease or on another day to drill a tube well. And mushrooming aid organizations come with ideas about how to improve their lives.

The changes can be seen in the way the people dress. More of the men wear trousers now. At festival time all the tribal women used to dress in simple, undyed cotton sarees and put flowers in their hair. Now they favour multicoloured, synthetic sarees. As they link arms to dance their traditional dance, the simplicity and unity that their white sarees appeared to symbolize has been replaced by vibrant, clashing colours.

Contact with the outside world has, for the most part, been detrimental to their way of life and brought more negative than positive results. As their poverty and the degradation of their natural environment is increasing, the supportive framework of community and culture is in decline.

24

The Sound of a Motorbike, the Beat of a Drum

Throughout the day on 25 April 1984 we kept hearing the distant sound of a motorbike, sometimes getting louder, sometimes receding. It is not a common sound in the villages. It usually heralds the arrival of a contractor. As it later turned out, the motorbike we heard that day was carrying the bidi-leaf contractor, Shri Rambilash Guturia.

In February and March many of the trees in the area shed their leaves and very soon new green ones begin to appear. It always surprised me that these new bright-green leaves should appear in the hottest season of the year, their greenness contrasting with the dry, brown earth. Amongst the new leaves to appear are the kendu or bidi leaves which are picked and dried to be made into bidis. It is from these leaves that Rambilash Guturia made money each year.

The diminishing forest where they were found belonged to the government which contracted out the collection of the leaves. This year there were four collecting points, called *khalyan*—one in our village, Fatepur, one in Jitpur about five miles westwards, one in Burhai about four miles to the north and one in Narasimor about ten miles away. There was a *munshi* in charge of each khalyan, usually a literate villager. The women left home, often before dawn, to go to the forest which could be far from their village. They picked the leaves in the scorching sun and hot wind. As the leaves were not very abundant it was a tedious job. They returned home around midday and then had to count them into bundles of fifty, twenty-five lying one way and twenty-five the other way. The bundles were packed and the women set off again to their nearest khalyan. There, they waited their turn to have their bundles counted after which they had to lay them out in the sun to dry. Sometimes the leaves were checked and some bundles were tossed away (and probably collected again later). They returned home after dark. That year the rate was four rupees per 100 bundles (that is, 5000 leaves) at two khalyans and four rupees and fifty paise at the other two (the reason for this difference escaped us). On an average one person could pick fifty bundles in a day which meant that the women were earning only two rupees a day. I believe the official daily wage at that time was eight or nine rupees.

Not surprisingly the women were not at all happy with this rate. We found this out by going to the khalyan and talking to them. First Manan went to our nearby khalyan on 27 April and the women there expressed their discontent to him very angrily. We decided to take up the matter for several reasons. The main one was, of course, that it was scandalous that the women should be exploited in this way. The villagers were facing such injustices in their lives every day. This seemed a good time to help them confront and overcome one such injustice. The bidi leaves had to be picked within a month or so. If the villagers didn't pick them no one else would. So, if they refused to pick them until the rate was increased they would certainly succeed. It seemed simple enough. This was only temporary employment and they would not starve if they stopped picking for a few days. They would manage somehow as they managed before the bidi leaf season and after it. All that was needed was a united effort.

On 28 April, our health workers, Somra and Shom, undertook a long trip by bicycle through the forest where the women were picking the leaves, visiting each of the khalyans. Another villager, Somlal, went with them of his own accord, leaving his other work, as he was very concerned. They set off at about 6 a.m. and didn't return until late in the evening. They felt that their efforts had been worthwhile as the response had been very good and it seemed that at least those women with whom they had talked had agreed to stop picking the leaves. The next day I went to our Fatepur khalyan to talk to the women there and to inform them that the women in other villages had decided to stop picking leaves. Manan and Shom went to the Burhai khalyan and again were encouraged by the response of the women. We had decided to call a meeting on 1 May at Karanpura village which was situated almost midway between the four khalyans. The purpose of the meeting was for the women to discuss what would be an appropriate rate. On 30 April only a very few women brought leaves to the Fatepur khalyan; most had stopped picking them.

It was very hot indeed on 1 May with a fierce wind blowing. After seeing patients all morning we set off. I was worried about taking Sushila who was nearly one year old, in such weather. Some of the women stopped me as we went through the village and also expressed their anxiety for her. I kept her covered as best I could but the wind sometimes made this difficult. Once we stopped, crouching down by a wall during a duststorm. After all this effort the meeting was disappointing. Somra had misjudged the situation when he thought that the meeting would be well attended. The women were not used to attending meetings. Hardly anyone came from other villages as we had hoped. One man, apparently drunk, was beating a drum and, every now and then, would interrupt by shouting slogans, some appropriate, some incomprehensible. He seemed to symbolize the absurdity and frustration of the situation. (There is something faintly absurd about an English woman with a baby talking to Indian villagers about the injustices done to them.) Some villagers were aroused enough to come with us afterwards to Burhai khalyan. There all the women we met claimed they didn't know the others had stopped picking leaves. By now the wind had dropped and Sushila enjoyed playing in the sand of a dry river bed.

The next day Manan and Toota went to Jitpur. It was a good thing they went for that very day the villagers had started delivering leaves again. They had been told that the rate had been raised to six rupees. We were annoyed that they had decided to start picking again without consulting the other villagers. However, when they went with Manan to the khalyan they found that the rate was still only four rupees. At this they were very angry and we were confident that that khalyan at least was well and truly closed. The villagers decided to call a meeting on the fifth. From Jitpur, Manan and Toota and two other villagers went to Narasimor. It was a long and tiring ride. As they approached they heard the sound of a drum. The Santhals beat their drums in a certain rhythm when they want to inform other villagers of some untoward event. Here, at the khalyan, was a solitary drummer protesting as the women brought their leaves. He was very much cheered by the unexpected arrival of four supporters.

The same day I went to the Fatepur khalyan and there I was shocked to find that a friend of ours, Sonomuni, whom we had treated for TB and who had been at the Karanpura meeting, was bringing leaves herself! At first I thought it couldn't be her, but as I approached I saw that indeed it was. She was confused to see me and tried to explain that the children had picked them. Some Fatepur women were also giving leaves, even some members of Somra's family! The next day more women started giving leaves again. We heard that at Burhai although all the Santhal women had stopped giving leaves, women of other castes continued to do so. Somlal was very angry. He came to me and told me to take down the names of all the women giving leaves and stop treating them! We could see the women taking leaves to the khalyan by a circuitous route, skirting around our house in the hope that we wouldn't see them. This made me feel very sad—as if we were against them! I wanted to at least explain to them what I felt. So in the evening Somlal and I went to call some villagers together for a meeting. It was heartening that they assembled very quickly. I explained that we were not there just to treat people's illnesses but to help them lead a better life and talked about the need to be united. It was sad for me, I said, to see that they were not yet ready for this and that they were happy to work all day for two rupees. They began to talk in a very animated way amongst themselves and then said that I was right. Tomorrow they would all go and close down the khalyan and seize the baskets of any women who brought leaves.

The next day, 4 May, I waited to see what would happen. But, as the shadows lengthened across the courtyard, no one appeared. It is true that no women were to be seen carrying baskets of leaves to the khalyan, but then no one appeared to be going to stop the women from the other villages either. Unable to contain my concern, I went into the village and could find no one about—a good number, including Somlal, had gone off to a wedding in a neighbouring village!

That evening there was the sound of the motorbike again. It passed our house in the darkness. Rambilash Guturia had come to buy a chicken with which to feed the mukhia. The mukhia, although himself a Santhal, was by now thoroughly corrupted—by chicken curry and other things. It was a sad and surprising fact that the villagers could be kept in a state of oppression for the price of a chicken and a bottle of mahua.

We had not succeeded in closing down the four khalyans as we had intended but we had been able to create some disruption for a few days, enough to cause Rambilash Guturia concern. Various rumours to upset our campaign had started. The mukhia was said to have threatened to report anyone who sounded the drums. Shivlal, the munshi at Fatepur khalyan who had also partaken of chicken curry, apparently said he would set alight the bundles himself if there was any trouble and then put the blame on the villagers. One villager told me he had heard that if the rate was raised the women would have to select the leaves whereas now they could pick all leaves, big and small. These threats and rumours were obviously absurd and indicate how easily the villagers are intimidated and confused. A more subtle way of counteracting our campaign was to refuse to pay the women the same day for the leaves they brought. They had to return the next day to collect their money and would bring more leaves when they came.

On 5 May there was a meeting in Jitpur. It was a good meeting, with villagers from the other villages present including the solitary drummer from Narasimor. It was planned that a march should take place from Jitpur to Narasimor the next day. However on the appointed day there was little active support and we decided to abandon the campaign. We called a meeting in Fatepur to explain our stand. In spite of our repeating that we had given up our efforts in the matter, the villagers declared that they would stop the collection of leaves at Fatepur. Several things had prompted this militant mood. One of the villagers had happened to go to Jitpur to visit a relative and had found the khalyan there closed, and had heard that in another place the rate was eight rupees. No doubt they too were feeling guilty for having broken their word earlier. The next day they went in force and closed down the khalyan. After that it began to rain intermittently for several days and the collection stopped anyway. When the weather cleared up the villagers were informed that the rate had been increased to five rupees and they accepted this and started picking leaves again. It wasn't much of a victory—it was more of an indication of what we could have achieved if the villagers had been united.

Our failure showed up the reality of village life—the general passive acceptance of injustice, the lack of unity, the relative ease with which one or two villagers are 'bought' by the exploiters to turn against the interests of their fellow villagers, and how easily the villagers can be misled and frightened. We were too few in number to cover such a large area and maintain the campaign. Although many of the women readily understood the situation and stopped picking leaves themselves, they did not take it upon themselves to talk to those who continued to do so. They simply went about their usual housework. Then, without further support and seeing others continue to pick leaves and earn a few paise, they too began to collect leaves again. Those like ourselves, Somra, Somlal and the solitary drummer were not able to maintain their motivation and confidence.

When they hear the sound of a motorbike arriving, the children rush out with shrieks of delight, full of curiosity. Little do they realize that it was bought with the help of their mothers' sweat!

25

Epilogue: Return to the Village

I returned to the village in the winter of 1998, twenty-four years after I had first arrived. Things had changed on the familiar train journey from Madhupur to Jagdishpur. A diesel engine has replaced the steam train and two new stops have been created, reflecting, no doubt, a larger population and greater movement.

Titmoh has changed too, almost beyond recognition. There was no sign of the house we had lived in. Apart from the bathroom and toilet, which had been built of brick, it has disappeared completely back into the earth. Tall leucena trees that we had planted now grow from what used to be the courtyard. The big mango tree is still there in all its splendour. But, nearby, Harpal's jackfruit tree is gone, making that part of the village look exposed and unfamiliar. I was told there had been a murder in a neighbouring village, and that Harpal's son and Hiro had been falsely accused and taken off to prison. The family had sold the tree to pay for their release. The well we used to collect water from has fallen in, but there are now three tube wells in different parts of the village.

More clumps of bamboo trees have grown, and to the north and east of the village there are now extensive acacia plantations. I am not an expert on soil conservation and the relative merits of different types of tree, but common sense would suggest that planting non-native species of trees over large areas was not a good idea. But then one does not have to venture far into the world of 'development' to realize that, all too often, common sense does not play a large part in it. The acacia plantation does, however, have some use for the villagers. The majority, rather to my surprise, are too scared to cut them down illegally, though a few gaps in the otherwise regular lines of trees suggest that some have been bold enough to do so. In March the fruit of the acacia trees is collected and sold to make shampoo in Calcutta, and in this way supplies a tiny seasonal income to a few villagers. Also, for a few weeks in the winter, the dry leaves are gathered, stuffed into sacks and taken home to be used as much-needed fuel for cooking.

One of our health workers, Somra, planted some of the leucena trees we had introduced near his home. Within a few years, they had grown both in height and girth to such an extent that they had supplied him with enough wood to build the elaborate roof of a large new house—with plenty to spare for window frames, doors and furniture. It puzzled me that more villagers had not followed his example; but then, he always had been one of the most enterprising. On this visit I found that he had bought some duck eggs and placed them under a hen. The one duckling that had successfully hatched was running along behind its 'mother' who didn't seem at all perturbed by the unusual appearance and sounds emanating from her new baby.

The jackfruit tree appears to be the most popular tree among the villagers, and grows surprisingly quickly when well cared for. Mahua saplings, on the other hand, seldom thrive and are prone to invasion by a particularly nasty beetle. Perhaps the disappearance of the jungle and lack of forest cover have rendered it more vulnerable.

The population of Titmoh appears to have doubled! Several new houses have been built. There are also three pukka

government buildings, a school, a community building and—
a hospital! But alas, there is nothing in the hospital. Baburam,
whose house in Jeromoh fell down, has been living there with
his family for the last six years. From the compound of the
community building rises a radio mast. There was even a
telephone, but only for a day because within twenty-four
hours someone stole it. (The idea of making a phone call
from Titmoh is mind-blowing. Earlier, even making a phone
call from Calcutta used to be a time-consuming and frustrating
experience.) The better-off villagers have, between them,
divided up beams from the now disused old school building.
I saw little sign of the kitchen garden, only a few remnants
of the brick wall that once surrounded it remain. The land
inside is level, the grass cropped. It would have made a good
football pitch! But the trees are still there and have grown
tall—mango, jackfruit and a solitary coconut tree which, I
was told, doesn't bear any fruit. Prabhu commented that it
might bear fruit if it was given some salt. I asked why he
hadn't tried it; he shrugged.

For some years there have been concrete posts—some
straight, some leaning at an alarming angle—along the
roadside. But there is no sign of the electricity they are intended
to convey. The dirt track has been reinforced at certain
treacherous places where it was in danger of being eaten up
by the encroaching erosion. No doubt this is for the benefit
of visiting government jeeps.

One significant change is the recent introduction of a new
variety of rice, 'tar rice', which, unlike the traditional variety,
doesn't need to be sown in a nursery and then transplanted.
It can be directly broadcast over the ground like wheat and
can grow on previously uncultivated land. The problem is
that it requires fertilizer. It has been heavily promoted and
the villagers are hooked. Some do express fears about the
long-term effect on the soil, and say it doesn't taste so nice.

The resulting reduction in the grazing lands and the neglect of traditional paddy and millet cultivation are also cause for concern.

The search for employment is as desperate as ever. Some opportunities have gone: the nearby stones for cutting are all but finished, kendu leaves are not collected any more and there are no more openings for casual workers in the coal mines. A few villagers have managed to secure permanent jobs there. Coal does provide employment locally for some living near Jagdishpur—selling coal that is. Every day you can see, at intervals along the road, men bent over pushing bicycles with an enormous load of coal lashed together and jutting out on either side. It is hard to believe that they push this load at least twenty miles from a coal mine in Giridih every day. The weight exceeds two hundred kilos. This monumental effort earns them about forty rupees a day. In the hot weather the effort involved is life-threatening. Indeed, I was told of a man whose bicycle got stuck in the sand of a stream he was trying to cross. His attempts to push it out literally split his back. Such is the struggle to earn a living just to survive.

The search for work extends further and further from home: now whole groups of men leave when the harvest is in to work in factories in Calcutta, two hundred miles away. This exodus is not altogether new. Bajoon is a very elderly resident of Fatepur. He was already a grandfather at the time of Independence and claims to be over a hundred years old. He remembers when Fatepur consisted of a mere twelve houses; now there are one hundred and fifteen. He describes how he used to work laying stones on railway lines for the British. Some of his contemporaries used to go to work in the paddy fields and coal mines of Bengal on foot, walking by day and sleeping under a tree at night. Nowadays the nature and scale of the exodus have changed. Contractors appear in the village to lure young men away, to work, for example, in cotton mills in the far-off states of Haryana and Gujarat. Very often this does not turn out as expected. The men receive food but no pay—the contractor who hires them disappears with the money he was supposed to use for salaries. When they realize they are trapped, they write home asking for help. But the replies sent from home are intercepted and never arrive at their destination. Some relatives raise money by selling their assets and animals to go and rescue their family member. It was explained to me how preparations for the escape are made by hoarding food beforehand. They leave under cover of darkness to make the long and difficult journey home. One villager told me with some amusement how a young man reappeared in the village after one and a half years, his hair and beard so long that he wasn't recognized!

Whether due to increased pressures caused by the growing population or the insidious influence of commercialization and an acquisitive society, or both, conflicts resulting in litigation are now commonplace, and the demands of dowry at the time of marriage negotiations are greater than ever. This is true even amongst the Santhals, who have not traditionally had a dowry system. Nor do the demands made on the bride's family stop with marriage. My friend Debimaya was not allowed to see her young daughter for nearly a year because she was not able to provide her son-in-law with a watch.

Madhupur itself is little changed. However, in front of the railway station, obscured somewhat by the crowds of people and mass of rickshaws, is the pleasant, rather incongruous sight of fountains surrounded by a garden of roses. Obviously Madhupur is trying to live up to its name (*madhu* means 'honey'). Along the roadside is the less happy sight of demolished structures—the result of government action against 'illegal' buildings and stalls. (It reminded me of Indira Gandhi's Emergency.) There are many more vehicles on the roads. The water tower is still not in use. The banyan tree that used to spread its branches over the vegetable market has been cut down and replaced by a concrete roof. The number of chemist shops has increased to an astonishing fifteen and the number of government doctors to ten, some of them working in a new hospital. They are mainly engaged in private practice and their presence has little impact on the villagers. Little has changed.

What has changed, however, is the number of NGOs that have cropped up. When we first began work in the village, we knew of no other groups working in the area. Now there has been an explosion of them. In Madhupur alone, I was told, there are about twenty and in neighbouring Deoghar forty! Many are no more than plaques on empty 'offices'. For, the first requirement of an NGO here is an office, preferably situated in a pleasant part of town with easy access for visitors. An impressive sign over the door is essential and the first crucial activity is the pursuit of FCRA (Foreign Contributions Regulatory Act)—the key that unlocks the door to foreign funds! Once this door is open, mastery of the language of development is the next prerequisite, that is to say, fluency in the use of terminology such as 'project proposal', 'feasibility study', 'target population', 'programme appraisal' and so on. When FCRA is secured and the funds start coming in you have to purchase office furniture (desks, filing cabinet, swivel chair, etc.) and arrange for letterheads to be printed. One essential item on the shopping list is a camera. This can be used to best effect during gatherings. An easy way to create such a photo opportunity is to call villagers together for a meal or a 'training session'. A large banner in English, proclaiming such a training programme, provides an eye-catching background for the photographs and ensures that there can be no doubt in the mind of the potential donor about what is going on. In this way the funds start rolling in and it is now time to purchase a motorbike. As the photographs and reports succeed each other, it is possible to progress to a jeep, and a driver. The speed at which this takes place depends on the level of expertise in 'Development Language'. As the organization expands, the purchase of vehicles, property and other 'visual' signs of success increases. Most of the desirable properties in one part of Jagdishpur have been bought up by one such organization.

I met a poor woman whose baby had an infected sore, probably the result of scabies. The baby had been given an injection by a quack and the woman showed me the vial with the rest of the medicine. The contents were to be used for a second injection the next day. She had been charged Rs 150. The vial appeared to contain only water. Neither the ten government doctors, nor the fifteen chemists, nor the twenty aid organizations had been much help to her.

I met Hiro, who had been at death's door with TB as a boy and is now a healthy and charming young man with a wife and a three-year-old daughter. It was a joy to see him. He supports his family by selling toddy from the date palms and by working as a labourer carrying heavy sacks in Giridih. And I met Indermani's wife, who once 'went mad' and now seems saner than many. She described, to the great amusement of her listeners, how she had attended one of the local NGOs' training sessions. At the end of it she had stood up and said, 'And now you can listen to me. Running after you and attending your meetings my hair has gone grey but it hasn't done me any good. While my situation is just the same it is you who have grown richer . . .' She told them the story (that we had related to her) of the big birds of prey who come and elicit the help of the crows to torment and feed off the little birds. The big birds were supposed to represent the moneylenders and rich landlords but in her mind they had become the NGOs. She had carried on in similar vein for some time and created quite a stir until the organizers, in disgruntled mood, started rolling up the mats and brought the proceedings to a close. She recounted the scene with great animation and had Debimaya in fits of laughter.

I met some of the poorest of my village friends for whom life is a never-ending struggle and yet they have somehow survived. Some whom I knew as malnourished children have, against the odds, grown into adulthood, married and had children of their own. I marvel at their endurance and resilience. At the same time I feel overwhelmed by the immense loss of all the latent talent, skill and accomplishment of so many millions of people, these inhabitants of another world who are denied the possibility of reaching their full potential. One glimpsed it in their innate skill, grace, artistry and physical stamina, but how much they might have been able to contribute to human knowledge and well-being will never be known.